Poems from Spain

Where shall we find you, George Brown?
We shall find you laughing in the mountains of Guadarrama
When we come back.
We shall find you at Teruel
When there's dancing in the streets.
We shall find you again in the streets of Madrid,
When Manchester and Brunete
And Villanueva de la Cañada have become
One and the same.
We shall come again, lorry after lorry, man after man,
In extended order, marching forward,
To find you where we left you,
Always George Brown.
Glory! What a day that'll be,
Wonderful, glorious,
What a day of wonder!
Every man will be a poet then
And every poet be free of his poetry;
Finding no song is made
For such a morning!

Anonymous

Poems from Spain

British and Irish International Brigaders on the Spanish Civil War

Edited by Jim Jump

¡ No pasarán!
Jim Jump

Lawrence & Wishart
LONDON 2006

ISBN 1 905007 39 6
British Library Cataloguing in Publication Data.
A catalogue record for this book is available from the British Library

Printed in Great Britain by Cambridge University Press

Contents

Members of the British Battalion's Anti-Tank Battery, including Miles
Tomalin (with recorder) and Hugh Sloan (crouching, bottom left).
Courtesy Stefany Tomalin

Foreword

Jack Jones

When Spaniards rose up to resist General Franco's military rebellion, it was an inspiration to millions of people across the world. The Spanish Republic held out for nearly three years and against all odds. It built an army from scratch and, with inferior weaponry, held back the tide of European fascism much longer than anyone could reasonably have expected.

Spanish democracy was ultimately defeated in 1939. But the heroic struggle of the Spanish people alerted the rest of the world to the threat of fascism. So did the savagery of Franco, whether it was the terror bombing of Madrid, Barcelona or Guernica, the deliberate shelling of refugees fleeing Málaga and Catalonia or the murderous repression of opponents in conquered parts of Spain. Such behaviour would soon be repeated by Franco's friends, Hitler and Mussolini, in the Second World War.

Like many other people at the time, I was deeply moved by the determination of most Spaniards to defend democracy and to stand up to fascism. Those of us who crossed the Pyrenees to help the Spanish Republic were convinced that this evil had to be stopped – and Spain was the place where this could be done. Otherwise, a wider European war was inevitable.

History proved us right and governments which had previously sat back and watched Spanish democracy being slowly bled to death were eventually forced to oppose fascism with arms and men. In the ensuing world war, which began only a few months after Franco's triumph, German Nazism and Italian fascism were crushed. Tragically, Spaniards had to wait three decades longer, until the death of their dictator in 1975, for democracy to return. But the Spanish people's part in checking the advance of fascism and in exposing its true nature played a crucial part in the victory of 1945.

It is fitting that the International Brigade Memorial Trust should sponsor this anthology of verse by the British and Irish International Brigade volunteers in that war. The poems are themselves memorials to that remarkable spirit of international solidarity which took 2,300 of us to Spain. All the raw passions and emotions which the Spanish Civil War produced – from idealism to despair, hope to anger, determination to fear – are found here in these poems. I hope they will continue to be read long after the last of the volunteers are gone and people will still ask: Who were these men and women? Why did they go? What did they see? What happened to them?

The International Brigade Memorial Trust

Proceeds of this book will go to the International Brigade Memorial Trust, which keeps alive the memory and spirit of the men and women who volunteered to join the legendary International Brigades to defend the Spanish Republic against fascism from 1936 to 1939.

The IBMT produces a regular newsletter and organises public events, including lectures and a national commemoration in Jubilee Gardens, London, in July of each year.

With an extensive archive on the volunteers from Great Britain, Ireland and the Commonwealth, the trust plays an important role in helping academics, researchers and educational establishments to find out more about the heroism and sacrifice of those who went to Spain. The trust's website [www.international-brigades.org.uk] reaches a wider audience throughout the world.

There are over 60 memorials in Britain and Ireland to the volunteers who went to Spain. Some take the form of impressive sculptures in our main cities, while others are simple plaques in public buildings or gardens. One of the key tasks of the trust is to ensure that these memorials are properly maintained.

Membership of the IBMT is open to all those who believe that the volunteers who decided that the cause of democracy in Spain was an ideal worth fighting for and, for many, dying for, are still an inspiration today.

Jack Jones is the President of the International Brigade Memorial Trust. He joined the British Battalion of the International Brigades in May 1938 as a twenty-five-year-old Liverpool docker and Labour local councillor. He was the political commissar of the battalion's No.1 'Major Attlee' Company and crossed the Ebro in July of that year in the Spanish Republic's Ebro offensive. Badly wounded in the shoulder during combat near Gandesa, he returned home in September after being discharged from hospital. He later become general secretary of the Transport and General Workers' Union.

Introduction

Jim Jump

Poetry is not expansion, it is compression, a coiled spring. It
is hard and spiky at the centre. In Spain everything was hard
and spiky and scraped the flesh.[1]

David Martin

Poems written by International Brigaders have appeared in antholo-
gies of Spanish Civil War verse; several Brigaders have had
anthologies of their own poetry published; at least four collections of
poems solely about the International Brigades have even been
produced in Spain. But, surprisingly for a war which has been
branded, however tendentiously, a poets' war, there has never been –
until now – an anthology of poetry written exclusively by those men
and women who went to Spain to help the beleaguered government
of the Republic between 1936 and 1939.

Thirty-three of the estimated 2,300 volunteers from Britain and
Ireland have poems in this collection. They were either soldiers of
the International Brigades or part of the medical services which
helped the war effort. Not all cases are clear-cut. Three poets
included in the anthology – Valentine Ackland, Ewart Milne and
Sylvia Townsend Warner – did not formally enlist with the
International Brigades or the Spanish Medical Aid Committee
(which were merged early in 1937), although they did undertake
work in Spain. Conversely, there are no poems by WH Auden,
Stephen Spender or others who made trips of propaganda value to
Republican Spain and of whom unsubstantiated claims have been
made of ambulance-driving, stretcher-bearing and even firing at
the enemy.

Six of the thirty-three gave their lives to the cause which took them
across the Pyrenees. Some were in Spain for many months and
survived successive battles and real hardship; others, for whatever

reason, could count their service in weeks. Most never regretted their decision to go to Spain; a few did change their minds about the war either at the time or later in life. No such distinctions or judgements have been made in selecting poems for this anthology. The poets are united here, as they were when they all chose to give practical meaning to their support for the Spanish Republic and their opposition to the rise of fascism in Europe.

International Brigader and poet Tony McLean described their mood:

> My generation had lived through the triumph of Hitler in Germany in 1933. We had seen German rearmament. We had seen the re-occupation of the Rhineland. We had seen Mussolini in Abyssinia. We had seen the defeat of the Austrian socialists in the Schutzbund uprising of 1934. All our foreign political experience was one of steady defeat as Hitler and Mussolini obviously were preparing for a second world war. We had no doubt that this second world war was coming. So when the Spanish resistance began in July 1936 we were all incredibly involved from the very first day.[2]

Every effort has been made to make this anthology as representative as possible of the cohort of International Brigade volunteers. So, poems by those individuals of whom it is not known whether they wrote any other verse have whenever possible been included, as have poems which have so far not appeared in any previous Spanish Civil War anthology. At the same time, many fine poems by the more prolific Brigaders, such as Clive Branson, Miles Tomalin and Tom Wintringham, have been left out for reasons of space and balance.

Why now? What is the point of bringing out an anthology of poems by soldiers and medics in a foreign war which began seventy years ago? First, it is the sad truth that all but a few International Brigaders have now passed into history, which means that it is possible to put together a collection which includes poems written not only during the war but also during the subsequent lives of veterans who continued to explore and describe their feelings and memories of Spain. Indeed, two of them, John Dunlop and David Marshall, died during the preparation of this book, for which they gave every encouragement and help. Secondly, the war, certainly in Spain, continues to cast a shadow over the politics and society of today. It remains a fierce battleground of ideas and historical interpretation, and some of the

Tom Wintringham (kneeling, left) and David Marshall (holding banner, right) in Barcelona in September 1936. *Courtesy Marlene Sidaway*

great political themes of the time – relations between church and state and devolution of power to the regions come immediately to mind – have resurfaced since the death of Franco in 1975. Most striking of all, the popular movement for official acknowledgement of the legitimacy of the Republic and the terrible crimes perpetrated against its supporters by Franco – embodied in the Asociación para la Recuperación de la Memoria Histórica (Association for the Recovery of Historical Memory) – has become one of the features of the Spanish political and cultural landscape since the turn of the last century. Remembrance, in a way which disturbs the so-called pact of silence – el pacto de silencio – that accompanied the transition to constitutional democracy in the late 1970s, is now a political act. This collection of poems can in its own way help that process. Here we commemorate those Spaniards who suffered because they loyally sided with the Republic and those British and Irish volunteers who recognised that the defence of Spanish democracy against fascism was their fight too. David Marshall reminds us in the anthology's final poem:

> Untrumpeted, their songs forgotten
> Our children are not taught their history.
> And you forget them at your peril ...

As for ordering the poems, thematic structures or a simple alphabetical listing of authors have been eschewed in favour of a narrative approach which loosely follows the course of the war and its aftermath both historically as well as at various personal levels. The result is that there are several overlapping but complimentary chronologies. With the help of the synopsis of the role of the British and Irish International Brigaders in the war on pages 123-134, the reader can, through successive poems, broadly trace the war's main battles and the shift in mood among participants from hope and idealism to recrimination, defeat and defiance. Then follows the Franco era and, with the generalísimo's death, the eventual restoration of democracy in Spain. For the individuals concerned, the war began and ended at different times. Some were arriving in Spain just as others were leaving, so poems written at different times during the war, but in which shared experiences are described, follow on from one another. Similarly, poems written many years after the event now stand alongside – and offer new perspectives on – those inspired in the moment of battle.

Eighty-five poems – not an exhaustive total – by thirty-three authors is a remarkable tally to extract from 2,300 individuals. A comparably representative anthology of verse written by combatants and auxiliaries in the Second World War would run to scores of volumes. Poems included here, of course, vary enormously in style and content. Works of great introspection and depth mingle with others which have come straight from the barrack room. There are agonisingly personal poems, songs of hope, laments for the dead, fist-clenching anthems and powerful political statements. Poets who went to war stand shoulder to shoulder with soldiers who penned a poem for the first and maybe last time. What they all share is the authenticity which firsthand experience brings to the poetic response to great historical events.

Just as significant is the number of working class volunteers who wrote poetry about their experiences. In contrast to the ordinary soldiers in the First World War, these men were part of the first truly literate working class generation. They were not conscripts, but exceptional individuals, activists for whom the labour movement – the Labour Party, trade unions, the Communist Party and its allied publishing, educational and cultural ventures – was a kind of university. Magazines like *Left Review, New Writing* and *Poetry and the People* consciously sought to publish working class poets and writers. In particular, they encouraged certain sorts of political poetry – freeverse and popular forms, poems for the stage as well as the page, poems rooted in direct experience rather than in ideological abstractions – all of which were suited to the exigencies of war poetry. Many of the poems to be read here enjoy a freedom from the constraints of traditional forms and diction, typically characterised by documentary detail and photographic imagery, first person plurals and present tense narratives, blunt language and anti-heroic gestures.

Taken as a whole, this collection serves to underline the significant role assumed by poetry in a war which, in WH Auden's well-known phrase, saw 'poets exploding like bombs'.[3] It would, of course, be easy to overstate the importance of poems and poets in a conflict which has also inspired great paintings and poster art, rousing speeches and slogans, fiction and journalism of distinction, along with memorable war photography and films. It must be said too that International Brigaders themselves have in general always been irritated by the 'poets' war' epithet, with its inference that the war was the preserve of intellectuals, thus obscuring the fact that more than 80 per cent of the volunteers from Britain were from the manual trades.[4]

And yet, there was surely something special about the place of poetry in the war. It is hard, if not impossible, to conceive of circumstances today in which a foreign war would provoke such an outpouring of verse in Britain and Ireland and, moreover, inspire so many poets and writers to take up arms. Why, then, did it happen in the case of Spain?

Was it because the great Spanish poets of the day – Rafael Alberti, Miguel Hernández, Federico García Lorca and Antonio Machado – had sided with the Republic and because Lorca had shockingly been murdered by the Francoists early in the conflict? Poetry, indeed, was deployed as a weapon of war and to stiffen morale, with Republican planes scattering copies of poems over Rebel troops and thousands of romanceros (poetic ballads) written and published in broadsheets to be sent to Republican trenches.[5]

Was it because in the 1930s writing and reading poetry constituted, as one critic has said, a kind of mass movement, specifically 'a movement of the passionate conscience'?[6] Catching the mood, the first issue of *Poetry and the People*, an offshoot of the popular Left Book Club, editorialised in July 1938:

> We begin to wield the weapon of poetry in the cause of the people, still perhaps a little unskilfully, but at last we have taken hold of the weapon with a firm hand, all doubts and fears dispelled. We have ceased to turn in on ourselves, we have passed the esoteric phrase.

Or was it simply because poetry was – and remains – such a democratic medium? Any literate person with pen and paper, even near the front line, could have a go. Many, as this anthology testifies, did so in Spain.

Most poets and writers in Britain and Ireland took it upon themselves visibly and loudly to defend the Republic. *Contemporary Poetry and Prose*, in tune with the times, devoted the whole of its back cover in September 1936 to declare: 'Support the Spanish People against Fascism' and continued its campaign in subsequent issues. Virginia Woolf – who was to lose a beloved nephew, the poet Julian Bell,[7] in the Spanish Civil War – wrote in the *Daily Worker* of 14 December 1936 that the artist was now forced to take part in politics, because: 'Two causes of supreme importance to him are in peril. The first is his own survival: the other is the survival of his art.'

Individual volunteers, the International Brigades themselves and their supporters in Britain all recognised the powerful appeal of poetry as a propaganda tool. *Volunteer for Liberty*, the International Brigades' English-language magazine published in Madrid and

Ewart Milne (left) and George Green (second from right) with a medical convoy for Republican Spain. Also pictured are Izzy Kupchick and Stephen Spender (third and fourth from left). *Courtesy Marx Memorial Library*

Barcelona, regularly featured poems translated from Spanish, plus poems written by volunteers. So did *The Book of the XV Brigade*, published in 1938 in Madrid.

Interestingly, author and journalist Ralph Fox[8] invoked William Wordsworth's notion of a 'spiritual community binding together the living and the dead' when he wrote about his decision to go to Spain:

> Our fate as a people is being decided today. It is our fortune to have been born at one of those moments in history which demand from each one of us as an individual that he make his private decision... We are part of that spiritual community with the dead of which Wordsworth spoke. We cannot stand aside. And by our action we shall extend our imagination, because we shall have been true to the passions in us.[9]

The passage was reprinted in the souvenir brochure produced for the rally in London on 8 January 1939 to welcome home the returning British Battalion. On its cover were Lord Byron's lines:

> Yet, Freedom! yet thy banner, torn, but flying,
> Streams like the thunder-storm against the wind.[10]

All this also suggests a perceived affinity between support for the Spanish Republic and the cause of 19th century Spanish liberalism which had been so enthusiastically embraced by the romantic movement of the day in Britain. [11]

> A glorious people vibrated again
> The lightening of the nations: Liberty
> From heart to heart, from tower to tower, o'er Spain,
> scattering contagious fire into the sky
> gleamed ...

Thus wrote Percy Bysshe Shelley in 'Ode to Liberty', celebrating the short-lived triumph of Rafael de Riego's liberal revolution of 1820.[12] Poet David Marshall, one of the earliest British volunteers, is described by fellow International Brigader – and Winston Churchill's nephew – Esmond Romilly as 'a boy of twenty-three' (in fact he was only twenty) who had brought copies of Keats, Swinburne and Shelly with him to Spain.[13]

Or was it something about the war itself which inspired so much poetry? After the moral ambiguities of the First World War, the rights and wrongs were clear enough: to defend a democratically elected and constitutional government against a fascist-backed military revolt aided by Hitler and Mussolini. There was plenty of ammunition here for poems of political advocacy and denunciation – of which there are several examples in these pages. Then there was the savagery of Franco and his allies: the deliberate shelling of civilian refugees, the indiscriminate bombing of towns and cities, the wave of terror in Rebel-held Spain in which tens of thousands of Republican sympathisers were summarily executed ... Even the murder of priests and nuns in those parts of Republican Spain where law and order broke down immediately after the 18 July 1936 military uprising – in which most of the Catholic Church sided with the Rebels – could not dim the enormity of Franco's crimes.[14]

Yes, all these crimes were soon to be eclipsed by the Blitz, Dresden, Hiroshima and the Nazi death-camps. But at the time, it was clear to most poets where their moral and creative duties lay:

> To many people the struggle of the Republicans has seemed a struggle for the conditions without which the writing and reading of poetry are almost impossible in a modern society.

So said Stephen Spender in 1939 and, in a tribute to the International Brigade volunteers, added:

Where the issues are so clear and direct in a world which has accustomed us to confusion and obscurity, action itself may seem to be a kind of poetry to those who take part in it.[15]

In the same spirit, C Day Lewis, in his homage to the International Brigades, 'The Volunteer', said:

> It was not fraud or foolishness,
> Glory, revenge, or pay:
> We came because our open eyes
> Could see no other way.[16]

As if to underline how clear the moral demarcation had seemed in the Spanish Civil War, the same poet would soon be asking, as the Second World War raged, 'Where are the War Poets?', and answering the title of his poem:

> It is the logic of our times,
> No subject for immortal verse –
> That we who lived by honest dreams
> Defend the bad against the worse.[17]

As Spender and Lewis seemed to acknowledge, it was the phenomenon of the International Brigades which also served to differentiate this war from others and to arouse the passions for which poetry was deemed to be the appropriate medium. By any standards, the mustering, for the most part clandestinely, of the International Brigades – some 35,000 volunteers from fifty countries – was an extraordinary event and achievement. Here was an act of unrivalled collective altruism, of international solidarity, of idealism put into practice and, given the fact that about a quarter of them lost their lives (including more than 500 of the 2,300 from the British Isles) – of astonishing bravery and self-sacrifice.

On 21 September 1938 before the assembly of the League of Nations in Geneva, the Spanish Republic's prime minister, Juan Negrín, announced the withdrawal of the International Brigades in a desperate attempt to reverse the non-intervention policy of the Western democracies. He said:

Spain will not forget either those who have fallen on their fields of battle or others who are still struggling. She is proud of their devotion and of their profound affection. I am sure that I am

not wrong when I say that before long their own countries will
feel equally proud of them, and that will be their best and great-
est reward.[18]

At the farewell parade in Barcelona on 28 October, Dolores Ibárruri,
'La Pasionaria', vice-president of the Cortes (Spanish parliament),
went further still:

> Comrades of the International Brigades. Political reasons,
> reasons of state, the welfare of that same cause for which you
> offered your blood with boundless generosity, are sending you
> back, some of you to your own countries and others to forced
> exile. You can go proudly. You are history. You are legend. You are
> the heroic example of democracy's solidarity and universality ...
> We shall not forget you, and when the olive tree of peace puts
> forth its leaves again, entwined with the laurels of the Spanish
> Republic's victory – come back! Come back to us. Those of you
> who have no country will find one.[19]

Decades passed before Negrín's prediction and La Pasionaria's
promise were fulfilled. It is easy to forget now how International
Brigade veterans were regarded in the postwar years. My own memo-
ries of childhood in suburban Kent in the 1950s and 60s were of my
father, James R Jump, having to conceal his war record in Spain to all
but family and like-minded friends. On his publisher's insistence, the
dust-jacket blurb on his first book[20] glossed over his involvement in
the war and coyly referred to 'the author of this book, who lived in
Spain for some years ...' Things were no doubt much worse for the
'premature antifascist' US veterans under the McCarthy witch-hunts
– or for those Brigaders who fell victim to Stalinist purges in some
East European countries – but there was still a general sense that
having fought on the side of the 'Reds' in Spain was cause for suspi-
cion. Indeed, my father, by now a Labour Party activist, but having
been a member of the Spanish Communist Party during the war, was
later to recount that the headmaster of a school in Rochester where
he had taught had confided to him afterwards that the county educa-
tion chiefs had passed on an instruction that an eye needed to be
kept on him for any suspicious political activities.[21]

If they were not dangerous lefties, then they must have been naive
fools. 'The betrayed idealists' bellowed the headline in the first of a
two-part feature in *The Sunday Times* of 23 July 1961 marking the 25th
anniversary of the start of the Spanish Civil War. Under photos of

International Brigaders, including Clive Branson (second from left), and two drivers on a campaign tour following their return to Britain. *Courtesy Marx Memorial Library*

Tom Wintringham, John Cornford and other prominent volunteers, the piece went on to explain that they had been betrayed – not of course by their own British government's shameful policy of non-intervention – but by the Soviet Union, one of only two countries to sell arms to the Republic (the other being Mexico).

Such was the official Cold War line, now that the Soviet Union was the enemy and there were reds under our beds, and the history of the Spanish Civil War was moulded to fit the new ideology. The Republic had been a victim of Stalinist skulduggery. That's what happens when you cosy up to Moscow. By extension, of course, the International Brigade volunteers had been Uncle Joe's dupes. After all, 60 per cent of them had been communists[22] and the International Brigades were the creation of the Comintern (Communist International).

Conscripted posthumously into this attack on the Republic and its supporters was the writer and journalist George Orwell (1903-1950) who, along with about twenty other Independent Labour Party supporters from Britain, fought with the militia of the far-left POUM (Partido Obrero de Unificación Marxista) party in Aragón early in the war. The brutal and mendacious way that the POUM and Anarchist militias in Barcelona were suppressed in May 1937 – in the not unreasonable bid to establish central government control over the war effort – and their members branded as traitors deserves to be condemned. But it was politically and historically perverse that the disillusionment felt by a former revolutionary socialist militiaman would so often and so effectively be deployed to hide Britain's culpability in abandoning the Republic.

Literary academics put the boot in too. Robin Skelton's introduction to *Poetry of the Thirties* asserted in 1964: 'It was clear that, far from being a struggle for democratic liberties, the civil war had become a military training ground for the Axis powers, and a pageant of propaganda for the Communists'. Hugh D Ford, who devoted a chapter to the 'poet-volunteers' in his 1965 survey of Spanish Civil War poetry,[23] said the 'dozen or so' poets 'had to believe that the ideal justified all the slaughter ... The cause, therefore, had the double duty of making suffering and death palatable and keeping the volunteers fortified for combat.' It would be difficult to disagree – indeed, George Green's anguished poem, 'Dressing Station', eloquently explores this moral dilemma – but it would be equally difficult to imagine the same tone of lofty cynicism applied to soldiers on, say, the Dunkirk or Normandy beaches. Valentine Cunningham, who used the poems of 15 volunteers in his 1980 anthology of Spanish Civil War verse, was only grudgingly more generous, at least to some of the International Brigaders, when he wrote that 'all the Stalinist lies, the politicking, the dodges and manoeuvres cannot dim the honour due to most of the volunteers. Sincerely and bravely they translated their faith into works.'[24]

Looking back at the sneers and insults that they faced, what is perhaps surprising is how few supporters of the Republic renounced what they did in and for Spain. Spender and Auden changed their minds. So did former student activist Philip Toynbee, who in 1976 would suggest that 'the Spanish war *can*, in the light of history, be roughly simplified into a war between communists and fascists',[25] apparently oblivious to the fact that the Republic had a liberal president, a socialist prime minister and the communists, though their influence and prestige had grown as a consequence of the help from the Soviet Union, were until the end in a minority in the cabinet. Ironically, Orwell, though he deplored the distortions of the truth he had witnessed in Spain, was never so dismissive of the Republican cause. He concluded that 'the broad picture of the war which the Spanish government presented to the world was not untruthful. The main issues were what it said they were'. Russian involvement in the war had been immensely exaggerated, he said. The outcome of the war had been settled in London, Paris, Rome and Berlin. 'The much-publicised disunity on the Government side was not a main cause of defeat.'[26]

Another great journalist who was in Spain during the war, Martha Gellhorn, never flinched in her support for the Republic and her disgust at the belittling of those who rallied to its defence. She wrote in 1959:

> I am tired of explaining that the Spanish Republic was neither a collection of blood-slathering Reds nor a cat's-paw of Russia. Long ago I also gave up repeating that the men who fought and those who died for the Republic, whatever their nationality and whether they were communists, anarchists, socialists, poets, plumbers, middle class professional men, or the one Abyssinian prince, were brave and disinterested, as there were no rewards in Spain. They were fighting for us all, against the combined force of European fascism. They deserved our thanks and our respect and got neither.[27]

Meanwhile, the Spanish people were denied the luxury of debating the rights and wrongs of the war which had devastated their country, killing up to half a million of them, exiling just as many and throwing an equal number into Franco's postwar gulag of prisons, concentration camps and slave labour battalions. Their fate, certainly for *los vencidos*, the defeated, resembled that of Germans under Hitler which International Brigader Christopher Caudwell described before his departure to Spain:

> No, let him work, and die if he protest,
> Gaoled without trial, or from sheer spite oppressed,
> Forbid to speak, to think, to read, to hear,
> Taught good by cruelty, courage by fear...[28]

Spaniards felt thrice betrayed. This I know from my mother, her family torn apart by the war, with her sister and brother also driven into exile from their native Basque country. First there had been the malevolent policies of non-intervention and appeasement by Britain which cleared the way for Franco's victory in 1939.[29] Then in 1945, after Franco had sent his Blue Division to Hitler's Eastern Front and while thousands of Republican exiles had fought to liberate Europe from fascism and thousands more had perished in Mauthausen and other Nazi concentration camps, the victorious Allies failed to insist on the restoration of democracy in Spain. Finally, during the Cold War, Franco's regime, not alone among murderous dictatorships around the world, invited the US to set up military bases and in doing so became Washington's anti-communist friend.

Historians will continue to argue about the role and legacy of the International Brigades and the wider pro-Republican Aid Spain movement. Were the British people roused out of the slumber of pacifism and alerted to the dangers of fascism? Did the mobilisation in favour of the Republic clear the ground for the popular war effort of 1939-1945? Was the eruption of support, which cut across traditional party political lines and social classes and which united trade unions, church groups, writers and artists, a forerunner of the great social movements of the 1960s and beyond?

My mother would recall how her hand trembled with emotion as she voted in 1945 in the expectation that a Labour government would do its best to topple Franco. For her, the International Brigaders from Britain did much to restore her faith in the decency of the British people which a dishonourable government had besmirched. 'Here we have shown to the world our country's other face', wrote Aileen Palmer in a poem about the German Thaelmann Battalion, a line which could as justly have been applied to the British volunteers. Go to Spain today and you will find plenty of people who endured the Franco era eager to say how grateful they were for the memory and example of those Britons and other Brigaders whose blood, in Rafael Alberti's words, could sing across frontiers.[30]

Half a century was a long time to wait – too long for the lives of many – but surviving International Brigaders in Britain would finally see the fulfilment of Negrín's and La Pasionaria's pledges – that they would in time receive proper recognition in their own countries and they would one day be welcomed home to Spain. In 1996, the Spanish government granted citizenship to the surviving veterans. Memorials have been erected to the volunteers in major towns and cities throughout Britain and Ireland, chief among them the imposing sculpture by Ian Walters on London's South Bank. It was unveiled in 1985, a year ahead of the 50th anniversary of the start of the civil war, which saw hundreds of veterans from around the world return to Spain and be cheered through the streets of Madrid. The same emotional scenes were repeated in Barcelona two years later.

Two memorials in Spain to British and Irish Brigaders deserve special mention. In Madrid there is a plaque in the Residencia de Estudiantes (Students' Residence), located behind the National Museum of Natural Sciences, which was unveiled in 1990 and is dedicated to five writers and International Brigaders who were killed in Spain. They include two poets, John Cornford and Charles Donnelly, who appear in this anthology, along with Julian Bell, Christopher Caudwell and Ralph Fox. Thus, the memory of them merges with the ghosts of the generation of renowned Spanish poets and artists, including Alberti, Lorca and Machado, who lived and studied at the Residencia. That generation, which will forever be associated with the Republic and the Spanish Civil War, was destroyed and dispersed by the same war which drew five young writers from the British Isles to Spain and their deaths.[31]

Nearly 300 miles away, on a hilltop high in the Sierra de Caballs near the village of Pinell de Bray, a plaque names the ninety British and Irish members of the British Battalion who lost their lives in the Ebro offensive between July and September 1938, the final battle of the war in which the International Brigades saw action. Among them are the poets Norman Brookfield and George Green. The unveiling ceremony in 2005 was notable for the presence of the British consul general in Barcelona and the military attaché from the embassy in Madrid.[32] It was the first time that there had ever been official recognition from HM Government of the role played by that remarkable volunteer army in Spain in the war against fascism which was soon to engulf the whole world.

Thanks

This anthology could not have been possible without the help of many people. Special mention must go to Marlene Sidaway, secretary of the International Brigade Memorial Trust, for her support and encouragement, along with the enthusiastic backing of other IBMT trustees, including Manus O'Riordan, who – as well as Ciaran Crossey – was a rich source of knowledge and advice on the Irish International Brigaders, and Richard Baxell, who allowed me to condense his online history of the British Battalion from the IBMT website. I am grateful to all those people who have made suggestions and supplied material for this collection, particularly relatives and friends of Brigaders: Rosa Branson, Joan Brown, Joseph Donnelly, Bob Edney, Martin Green, Juanita Jolly, Kathy Lee, Margaret McLean, Michael O'Brien and Stefany Tomalin. Invaluable help was provided by Jim Carmody in piecing together biographical information on Brigaders from the archive held by the IBMT. Hugh Purcell alerted me to the existence of previously unpublished poems by Tom Wintringham. Antonio Díez assisted with research at the Working Class Movement Library, Salford. Thanks must also go to the ever helpful staff at the Marx Memorial Library in London, repository of the International Brigade Memorial Archive, and at the Imperial War Museum Sound Archive, London. I am grateful too to Sally Davison of Lawrence & Wishart for pursuing this project with such zest, Andy Croft for his editorial comments and Eva López Cabello for checking the Spanish. Myra, Clara and Meirian gave unstinting support, and put up for over a year with my obsession with these poets and poems. Finally, I am grateful for all the help and kind words of the surviving International Brigaders, especially IBMT trustees Jack Jones, Jack Edwards and Sam Lesser[33] and poets John Dunlop and David Marshall, who sadly died before publication. This book is a memorial to them and their comrades who went to Spain in 1936-1939.

Notes

1. From *My Strange Friend*, by David Martin, Pan Macmillan, Sydney 1991.
2. Tony McLean, Imperial War Museum Sound Archive, London.
3. From the poem 'Spain', published as a pamphlet by Faber & Faber (London 1937), with proceeds going to Spanish Medical Aid.
4. See analysis of Brigaders' occupations in *British Volunteers in the Spanish Civil War: The British Battalion in the International Brigades, 1936-1939* by Richard Baxell, Routledge/Cañada Blanch Studies on Contemporary Spain, London 2004.
5. Quoted in Cary Nelson's introduction to *The Wound and the Dream: Sixty Years of American Poems about the Spanish Civil War*, University of Illinois Press, Chicago 2002.
6. See Robin Skelton's introduction to *Poetry of the Thirties*, Penguin Books, Harmondsworth 1964.
7. Julian Bell was born in Bloomsbury, London, in 1908 and taught at Wuhan National University, China, from 1935 before going to Spain in June 1937 as an ambulance driver. He died from wounds received in an air attack at Brunete on 18 July 1937.
8. Ralph Fox was born in Halifax in 1900 and read modern languages at Oxford. He was a founder member of the Communist Party and enlisted with the British Battalion in December 1936, becoming a battalion assistant political commissar. He was killed on 28 December 1936 while on reconnaissance near Lopera on the Córdoba front.
9. From *The Novel and the People* by Ralph Fox, Lawrence & Wishart, London 1937.
10. From 'Childe Harold's Pilgrimage'. The same lines are inscribed on the International Brigade memorial in Jubilee Gardens in London's South Bank.
11. For a lively description of the romantic movement's attachment to

The British Battalion's banner being paraded through the streets of Barcelona in November 1988 when hundreds of veterans from around the world gathered in the city to mark the 50th anniversary of the passing-out of the International Brigades. *Photo: Andrew Wiard*

Spanish liberalism, see Tom Burns Marañón's *Hispanomanía*, Plaza & Janés, Barcelona 2000.

12. Riego was executed in 1823. The 'Himno de Riego' ('Riego's Hymn') became the anthem of the Spanish Republic.

13. See account in *Boadilla* by Esmond Romilly (Hamish Hamilton, London 1937). Romilly, born in London in 1918, arrived in Spain in October 1936, joining a unit with other British volunteers in the mainly German Thaelmann Battalion, and took part in action around Madrid at Cerro de los Ángeles, University City, Casa de Campo and Boadilla del Monte. He was repatriated in January 1937 but returned to Republican Spain as a reporter for the *News Chronicle* in the following month with Jessica Mitford, with whom he was married in Bayonne in France. He volunteered for the Royal Canadian Air Force in 1939 and died when he was shot down over Germany in 1941.

14. See *The Crimes of Franco*, the 2005 Len Crome Memorial Lecture by Paul Preston (International Brigade Memorial Trust, London, 2005), in which Preston calculates that between 1936 and 1945 approximately 180,000 Spaniards were executed with or without trial by Franco and his agents.

15. From *Poems for Spain*, edited by Stephen Spender and John Lehmann, The Hogarth Press, London 1939.

16. First published in *Overtures to Death*, by C Day Lewis, Jonathan Cape, London 1938. 'Our open eyes could see no other way' is one of the inscriptions on the International Brigade memorial in London's Jubilee Gardens.

17. From *The Complete Poems of C Day Lewis*, Sinclair-Stevenson, London 1992.

18. Quoted in *Britons in Spain* by William Rust, Lawrence & Wishart, London 1939.

19. Quotation taken from the bound copy of La Pasionaria's speech 'Hasta pronto hermanos / Goodbye brothers, till our speedy reunion / Frères, à bientôt' which was handed to all International Brigaders before leaving Spain.

20. *The Spaniard and his Language*, by JR Jump, George G Harrup, London 1951.

21. James Jump, Imperial War Museum Sound Archive, London.

22. See breakdown of political affiliations in *British Volunteers in the Spanish Civil War: The British Battalion in the International Brigades, 1936-1939*, op. cit.

23. *A Poets' War: British Poets and the Spanish Civil War*, by Hugh D Ford, Oxford University Press, London 1965.

24. From *The Penguin Book of Spanish Civil War Verse*, edited by Valentine Cunningham, Penguin Books, Harmondsworth 1980. For a coruscating critique by a historian of Cunningham's introduction to the anthology, see John Saville's 'Valentine Cunningham and the Poetry of the Spanish Civil War', in *The Socialist Register 1981*, edited by Ralph Miliband and John Saville, Merlin Press, London 1981.

25. From 'Journal of a Naive Revolutionary' in *The Distant Drum: Reflections on the Spanish Civil War*, edited by Philip Toynbee, Sidgwick & Jackson, London 1976.

26. See Orwell's *Looking back on the Spanish War* (New Road, London 1943), in which was also published his only poem directly inspired by Spain: 'The Italian soldier shook my hand'.

27. From *The Face of War*, by Martha Gellhorn, Hart-Davis, London 1959.

28. From the 1935/6 poem 'Heil Baldwin!', published in Caudwell's *Collected Poems 1924-1936*, edited by Alan Young, Carcanet Press, Manchester 1986. Caudwell (real name Christopher St John Sprigg) was born in Putney, south London, in 1907, and was the author of several books on poetry and on aeronautics, as well as being a crime fiction writer and a reporter for the *Yorkshire Observer*. He was living in Poplar, east London, when he volunteered for Spain in November 1936, travelling as a driver with a convoy of medical supplies. He joined the No.2 Machine Gun Company of the British Battalion in the following month and was killed on 12 February 1937 during the battle of Jarama.

29. See *La perfidia de Albión: El gobierno británico y la guerra civil española*, by Enrique Moradiellos (Siglo XXI de España Editores, Madrid 1996), which shows how non-intervention was not founded on the principle of genuine neutrality, but rather on a policy deliberately aimed at securing Franco's victory.

30. See Alberti's poem 'A las Brigadas Internacionales' ('To the International Brigades'); first published in *Nuestro Ejército* (18 September 1937); reprinted in *Voluntarios de la libertad: 50 poemas sobre las Brigadas Internacionales*, edited by Severiano Montero Barrado, Asociación de Amigos de las Brigadas Internacionales, Madrid 2001.

31. Lorca was murdered by the fascists in Granada in August 1936; Machado died in a refugee camp in Collioure, France, in February 1939; Alberti left Spain in 1939 for exile in Paris, Buenos Aires and Rome, returning to Spain in 1977 and dying 12 years later. The other renowned poet of the 'Generación del 27', Miguel Hernández, died in a Franco gaol in Alicante in March 1942 after his death sentence had been commuted to 30 years imprisonment.

32. See full report in *IBMT Newsletter* of June 2005.

33. Jack Edwards, born in Liverpool in 1913, worked as a motor mechanic before arriving in Spain in January 1937. He served with the British Battalion at the battle of Jarama, where he was wounded, and afterwards joined the 1st Transport Regiment and later the 129th Artillery Division. He saw action at Teruel, Aragón and the Ebro, finally returning to Britain in January 1939. Sam Lesser, born in London in 1915, was an Egyptology student at University College, London, when he travelled to Spain in September 1936. He was assigned to the Commune de Paris Battalion and fought in the defence of Madrid at University City, Casa de Campo, Pozuelo and Boadilla. He transferred to the La Marseillaise Battalion and was wounded in late December at Lopera on the Córdoba front. He was repatriated in February 1937 but returned to Spain in July and was involved in press and propaganda work until December 1938.

THE FREEDOM OF ~~CRITICAL~~ THE CITY

The freedom of Guernica has been conferred on Generalissimo Francisco Franco.

Through the undisputed heaven,
Bent on hopes of greater glories
Than the ~~brittle promise could~~ had given
Came the fascist trimotors,
On Guernica loosed their venom,
Hammered helpless men & women
Into the ~~pulped~~ and writhing earth ~~oh~~.
~~And~~ ~~blitz to birth.~~
~~Thus they stamped the~~

Gaudily across the passes
Now no longer barricaded,
White hope of the ruling classes
Since all other hopes have failed,
Franco rides ~~with pomp and~~ pageant,
Little salesman, ~~foreign~~ agent,
Rides between the flags and vistas
Staged by anxious Falangistas
To receive the freedom ordered
From the city that he murdered.

Eyes in all the darker places,
~~Round~~ the door, behind the pillar,
~~E~~ Only eyes, never faces,
Eyes ~~rebelled~~ at the killer.
Now the germ of panic's stirring
~~Where's~~ ~~They~~
~~Hitler~~ ~~so did Goering~~
~~to complete the story~~
~~Eyes that~~ ~~the face of~~
~~Have the freedom of a city~~
~~Ten years dead and gone to offer.~~

tyrants' deaths are equalled, gory
Mussolini, Hitler, Goering
there in eyes that ...
... read the final chapter
Now within the murdered city
freedom waits to greet her ...

Scorched, and ~~splintered~~ lie its stones,
~~...~~ flesh and hair,
~~...~~ bones —
El Caudillo's welcome there.
There the friendly maggot fêtes him
With his pomp and pinchbeck fasces,
There the ~~city's~~ freedom waits him
Where he left its dust and ashes.

A draft of Miles Tomalin's poem 'Aftermath'. *Courtesy Stefany Tomalin*

The poems

Clive Branson

December 1936, Spain

You! English working men!
Can't you hear the barrage creeping
that levels the Pyrenees?

Is time intangible
that bears so audible
and visible a thing?

Can't you hear the children and women cry
where the Fascist bomb
makes the people's home
a tomb for you and me?

Can't you see the gashes in the street
where our people stumble
when the city trembles?
Can't you smell the rose held in their teeth
tighter than death?
Silent they lie
with no Cross
only this
their courage, their faith
manures the barren earth
for new trees
to spring up the hill-side to the very sky.

That we should not hear at such a time
makes deafness and peace the bloodier crime.

Written 16 June 1939

Miles Tomalin

Alès

Daring closely even this urban circle
Nightingales chant, the darkwood night
Is inlaid with ivory song, while
Towards the white air of tomorrow
Rises in slow spiral the sleep of thirty men.
All the floor's a bed,
The straw, the smell, the kaleidoscopic cockroaches
Never ravel the curtain of their snores.
Lying here, your lovers and your haters
Are not the men, those men, you knew,

The nightingales throw music over the hour's edge
In falls of ambling volume: they'll outlive the town
To be for many thousand years the same
As on those thousands of midnights falling
Before Keats heard their enchanted summons.
We, within our short tomorrow,
Will have climbed into the violent ring of powder
Among guns' stream of venom and saw-edged fighting moods,
There where there's a new world's door to knock on.

These men are proud,
Not all the world, though it knows a nightingale,
Knows us who hear above all songs
The steps of an old world going.

May 1937

Tony McLean

Sunrise in the Pyrenees, May 1937

Once looking west in ecstasy of daring
we saw the future pegged out like a sheet
its mountains, towns and valleys at our feet
yet lacked a map to give them name or bearing
from in our souls followed the lodestone here

old Orpheus' lyre compelled our feet to Spain
and set our veins afire, useless to explain
this was our summit, peak of our hearts' career.
Forty the years Moses trudged willingly
to view his Canaan from Mount Nebo's height
while our apocalypse with eager light
red rising sun revealed in ecstasy.
What if rash hopes turned ash in burning Spain?
Yet we who have climbed up have not climbed in vain.

Valentine Ackland

Badajoz to Dorset, August 1936

Telephone wires cry in the wind
& make song there. I stand in the misty night
& listen. Hear voices from a far distance
hear sounds from further, outside the wires,
than ever inside. Hear sounds from Spain.
The mist muffles all but these; blankets perhaps the reply –
but the wind plays the wires still, & the wires cry.

Eric Edney

Salud!

Men of all lands from field and factory sped,
United in purpose, but of that purpose dumb
To one another till Spain welcomed them,
And, understanding, each man thither come
First heard the word: Salud!

A nation's mighty purpose in one word
That moment showed; and each one felt his heart
Uplifted, and his will and arms more strong,
And in the struggle played a worthier part
For hearing that: Salud!

A machine-gun suddenly a whistling chain
Projects, and Death hurtles perilously by;
We raised clenched fists high in the riven air,
Taunting defiant, and ironic cry
The single word: Salud!

Black figures looming beneath the olive trees
Dig shallow graves for the heroic dead;
Plant two crossed laths of ammunition-box,
Bearing no eulogy, above their head,
But just one word: Salud!

This is no mystery, and needs no priest
To guarantee us victory over Death.
That word itself bears witness, time to come
Men 'neath whatever heaven drawing breath
Shall cry to life: Salud!

Sylvia Townsend Warner

Journey to Barcelona

In that country pallor was from the ground,
darkness from the sky.
As the train took us by
we debated if it were mountain we saw or cloud.

The bleached fields are pallid as truth might be.
Men move on them like clouds.
Dwellings like hempen shrouds
wrap up squalor with a grave dignity.

Pale is that country like a country of bone.
Dry is the river-bed.
Darkness is overhead,
threatening with the fruitfulness implicit in storm.

The willows blanch, and catch their breath ...
It rains in the hills!
The parched river-bed fills,
the sky thunders down fruitfulness.

Faithful to that earth the clouds have gathered again.
If the profile unknown
were cloud, it will be storm
before long. Rain from the red cloud, come to Spain!

John Cornford

Full Moon at Tierz: Before the Storming of Huesca

1
The past, a glacier, gripped the mountain wall,
And time was inches, dark was all.
But here it scales the end of the range,
The dialectic's point of change,
Crashes in light and minutes to its fall.

Time present is a cataract whose force
Breaks down the banks even at its source,
And history forming in our hands
Not plasticene but roaring sands
Yet we must swing it to its final course.

The intersecting lines that cross both ways,
Time future, has no image in space,
Crooked as the road that we must tread,
Straight as our bullets fly ahead.
We are the future. The last fight let us face.

2
Where in the fields by Huesca the full moon
Throws shadows clear as daylight's, soon
The innocence of this quiet plain
Will fade in sweat and blood, in pain,
As our decisive hold is lost or won.

All round, the barren hills of Aragon
Announce our testing has begun.
Here what the Seventh Congress said,
If true, if false, is live or dead,
Speaks in the Oviedo mauser's tone.

Three years ago Dimitrov fought alone
And we stood taller when he won.
But now the Leipzig dragon's teeth
Sprout strong and handsome against death,
And here an army fights where there was one.

We studied well how to begin this fight.
Our Maurice Thorez held the light.
But now by Monte Aragón
We plunge into the dark alone,
Earth's newest planet wheeling through the night.

3
Though Communism was my waking time,
Always before the lights of home
Shone clear and steady and full in view –
Here, if you fall, there's help for you –
Now, with my party, I stand quite alone.

Then let my private battle with my nerves,
The fear of pain whose pain survives,
The love that tears me by the roots,
The loneliness that claws my guts,
Fuse in the welded front our fight preserves.

O be invincible as the strong sun,
Hard as the metal of my gun,
O let the mounting tempo of the train
Sweep where my footsteps slipped in vain,
October in the rhythm of its run.

4
Now the same night falls over Germany
And the impartial beauty of the stars
Lights from the unfeeling sky
Oranienburg and freedom's crooked scars.
We can do nothing to ease that pain
But prove the agony was not in vain.

England is silent under the same moon,
From Clydeside to the gutted pits of Wales.
The innocent mask conceals that soon

Here too our freedom's swaying in the scales.
O understand before too late
Freedom was never held without a fight.

Freedom is an easily spoken word
But facts are stubborn things. Here, too, in Spain
Our fight's not won till the workers of all the world
Stand by our guard on Huesca's plain,
Swear that our dead fought not in vain,
Raise the red flag triumphantly
For Communism and for liberty.

Frank Brooks

'Like molten gold the sun on high'

Like molten gold the sun on high
Purples the mists of the far off hill:
Beauty dwells in palm and sky,
You are lovelier still.

O'er Teruel, the mountains frown
And eye and mind in vain beguile,
To gain a moment's high renown,
To match the sweetness of your smile.

La Mancha's plains with glee can sing,
Your rosy cheeks are the same proud hue
And wines and spice in tribute bring,
Rejoicing to resemble you.

A trio of things I can declare:
The young palm's green and the wind is free,
And you are lovely beyond compare –
And I, alas, love thee.

Thomas O'Brien

Beauty Is Found To Be Ugly

Beauty is found to be ugly
Only on the surface;
Like a ripe orange it needs peeling
Which, fingers clumsy,
Squirts juice and splits and warps:
A messy way.
Because we are stupid
Having learned little that matters
It is found in obscurity;
Crawls like crab under weed.
Weed and crab must be found and lifted
And underneath it is found,
The tender place, underneath.

A man cannot see beauty
And afterwards destroy it
Without destroying himself;
Content with what he sees
Will he pluck out his own eyes
To die in darkness and loneliness?

When will people start admiring each other
And cease torturing themselves?
My mother will put in a good word for me;
Haven't you a mother or a father who will
    put in a good word for you?

In Spain
Lunn-sped shells splinter the bones of children
And old people seeking nothing but the slant of peace
Every day sludge the ground in sudden gore
Because they had lately seen
A little beauty under the ugliness.

Under such trying conditions
Must we advance to a better life?
Well, then, we must.
Certain it is
We shall not pluck out our own eyes.

1937

Clive Branson

The International

We'd left our training base
And by the time night fell
Stood facing the Universe
Singing the 'International'.

I remember it so well
Waiting in the station yard
The darkness stood around still
And the stars, masses, stared.

That's when I first understood
One is never alone in this fight.
I'd thought the 'good-bye' was for good
And left *all* behind that night.

But everything new that I meet
No matter how strange and uncertain,
Holds something familiar that
Proves the fight is still on.

How often I've marched, and marching
I sang of an England unseen,
Watched the great crowds gathering
And the tramp of their feet beat in tune.

Even in the grip of prison
I joined in the singing of millions
As they wait at their wayside station
That leads to the battle lines.

I'm singing in every country
Where I tread through the streets of Time,
One man, one woman, humanity,
The 'International' our theme.

January 1940

Anonymous

The Internationalist

Ich came nach Spain in Januar
Yo hablar seulement English,
But jetz I say Comment Savar,
Wie gehts, Que tal, tovaritsch.

Ich faren mit mein ambulance
In woikin shoit and panties,
No tengo tiempo por romance,
Y arbeit más duro que antes.

Wen abend komt, I say BON Soir,
Mi convertures alles veloren,
Ich bin sehr kalt, but I am told
C'est la guerre, dasder krieg, there's a war on.

But underer dings Ich hat gelernt
That mange ist nicht veel,
Nosotros fleisch is sometimes burnt,
Mit garlis, también huile.

Pero, una idea es uber alle,
An idea muy profundo,
We'll arbeit schwer for Franco's fall,
Und U.H.P. en todo el mundo.

John Cornford

A Letter from Aragon

This is a quiet sector of a quiet front.

We buried Ruiz in a new pine coffin,
But the shroud was too small and his washed feet stuck out,
The stink of his corpse came through the clean pine boards
And some of the bearers wrapped handkerchiefs round their faces.
Death was not dignified.
We hacked a ragged grave in the unfriendly earth
And fired a ragged volley over the grave.

You could tell from our listlessness, no one much missed him.
This is a quiet sector of a quiet front.
There is no poison gas and no H.E.

But when they shelled the other end of the village
And the streets were choked with dust
Women came screaming out of the crumbling houses,
Clutched under one arm the naked rump of an infant.
I thought: how ugly fear is.

This is a quiet sector of a quiet front.
Our nerves are steady; we also sleep soundly.

In the clean hospital bed my eyes were so heavy
Sleep easily blotted out one ugly picture,
A wounded militiaman moaning on a stretcher,
Now out of danger, but still crying for water,
Strong against death, but unprepared for such pain.

This on a quiet front.

But when I shook hands to leave, an Anarchist worker
Said: 'Tell the workers of England
This was a war not of our own making.
We did not seek it.
But if ever the Fascists again rule Barcelona
It will be as a heap of ruins with us workers beneath it.'

Tom Wintringham

Spanish Lesson

Young men marching, gallant Spanish fashion,
The free arm swinging across and elbow high,
Are Spain's new bread and wine,
The blood of new Spain's passion,
The body of our sacrifice;
Vino y pan.

Their gesture as they march is that of the peasant
Scattering the rough grain that shall be your bread;
And our hunger, desire
For the grape-breasted vine,
Is Spain's past year and present:
Hambre y sed.

After harvest, after victory, we shall be forgotten
As men forget seed-grain, harrowing, dung –
Blood of wounds gone rotten –
But hope is down the path
Of the young men marching:
Guerra – y paz.

August 1937

Joe Monks

Fuente-O-Venjuna

Remember long ago, Fuente-O-Venjuna
A laddie whispered low: Fuente-O-Venjuna.
Will I stay or will I go?
And you proudly answered go!
It were better to lay a tyrant low
Than live a slave without a blow, for Fuente-O-Venjuna.

Bill Harrington

Marching Song of the 2nd Company of the British Battalion

D'ye ken the traitor Franco
Whose hair is turning grey?
D'ye ken the traitor Franco
Whose had his little day?
D'ye ken the traitor Franco?
He's fading away
As the day of the workers is dawning.

For the sound of our voices
Have filled him with dread,
And the clamour of the people
Has endangered his head,
And soon the poor fellow'll
Be wishing he was dead
For the day of the workers is dawning.

Yes we ken the traitor Franco
And his motley crew:
Queipo and Musso
And the paper-hanger too,
From defence to attack,
From attack to the kill,
As the day of the workers is dawning.

Yes we ken the traitor Franco,
Who's found he could not stay.
He lived at Burgos
One on a day,
But now he has gone
Far, far away,
For he fled to Salamanca in the morning.

Tom Wintringham

International Brigades

Men are tied down, not only by poverty,
By the certain, the usual, the things others do,
By fear for and fear of another. Liberty
Is a silly word, in this flat life, and used
Usually by a Lord Chief Justice. It smells of last century.
There are free men in Europe still:
They're in Madrid.

Men are so tired, running fingers down football tables
Or the ticker-tape, or standing still,
Unemployed, hating street-corners, unable
– Earth-damned, famine-forced, worn grey with worklessness –
To remember manhood and marching, a song or a parable ...

While the free men of Europe
Pile into Madrid.

Men who could not be broken even by Hitler's prisons,
Rubber truncheon, police spy, surrender of friends,
From the Lipari islands, from the divisions
Roadmaking in French Morocco under the sun;
And from comfort, good wages, home – each of them made his
    decision

The free men of Europe, not yet ten thousand,
Raid forward from Madrid.

Forming today the third of the brigades, equipping Italians,
Frenchmen, Germans, Poles, Jugo-Slavs, Greeks,
– The names mean languages only: these are Europeans –
The staff, corduroy-trousered, discuss when Franco will use it:
'Two weeks' or 'a month yet'? How many gas-masks by then?
Will Europe, will England, will you 'have given the gas-masks'
For the free men of Europe
Entrenched in Madrid?

Estado Mayor, Brigada Internacional 28.11.36

George Green

Dressing Station

Casa de Campo, Madrid, March 1937

Here the surgeon, unsterile, probes by candle-light the embedded
    bullet.
Here the ambulance-driver waits the next journey; hand tremulous
    on the wheel, eye refusing to acknowledge fear of the bridge, of
    the barrage at the bad crossing.
Here the stretcher-bearer walks dead on his feet, too tired now to
    wince at the whistle of death in the black air over the shallow
    trench; too tired now to calculate with each journey the
    diminishing chances of any return to his children, to meals at a
    table, to music and the sound of feet in the jota.

Here are ears tuned to the wail of shells: lips that say, this one gets the whole bloody station: the reflex action that flings us into the safer corners, to cower from the falling masonry and the hot tearing splinters at our guts.

Here the sweet smell of blood, shit, iodine, the smoke-embittered air, the furtive odour of the dead.

Here also the dead.

Here also the dead.

This afternoon five.

Then eight.

Then two neat rows.

And now ... this was the courtyard of the road-house, filling-station for the Hispano-Suizas and the young grandees' bellies. The sign American Bar still hangs unshattered.

... I cannot count. Three deep: monstrous sprawling: slid from dripping stretchers for more importunate tenants: bearded plough-boys' faces: ownerless hand: shattered pelvis: boots laced for the last time: eyes moon-cold, moon-bright, defying the moon: smashed mouth scaring away thought of the peasant breasts that so recently suckled it ...

I cannot count.

But poet, this is old stuff.
This we too have seen.
This is Flanders 1917. Sassoon and Wilfred Owen did this so much better.
Is this all?
Do twenty years count for nothing?
Have you no more to show?

Yes, we have more to show.

Yes, though we grant you the two-dimensional similarity, even (to complete the picture) allowing you the occasional brass-hat and the self-inflicted wound.

Yet there *is* another dimension. Look closely. Listen carefully.

Privilege here battles with no real privilege.

The dupe there, machine-gunning us from the trenched hillside, fights still to preserve a master's title-deeds, but we ... we battle for *life.*

This ... we speak a little proudly, who so recently threw off the slave shackles to do a man's work ...

This is *our war.*

These wounds have the red flag in them.
This salute carries respect.
Here the young soldier says 'camarada' to his general.
Here we give heed to no promise of a land fit for heroes to live in, but take for ourselves the world to mould in our hands.
These ranks can never be broken by four years of mud and bitter metal, into sporadic and betrayed rebellion.
Here the consciousness of a thousand years' oppression binds us as brothers ... We have learnt our lesson.
Look. Over the bridge (it is not yet dawn) comes a Russian lorry, ammunition-laden.
Forty-three years gone, unarmed St Petersburg's blood paid a heavy duty on those shells.
And I? The Chartists commandeered this ambulance from a Portland Street shop-window.
I drove: and dead Communards raised living fists as far south as Perpignan. I saw the perils of the Pyrenees spurned by feet that once had scaled a Bastille, by the fair-haired boys who graduated in the streets of Charlottenburg, by those who paid a steerage passage, to tell us how their fathers fell at Valley Forge.
For this is not 1917.
This is the struggle that justifies the try-outs of history.
This is the light that illuminates, the link that unites Wat Tyler and the Boxer rebellion.
This is our difference, this is our strength, this is our manifesto, this our song that cannot be silenced by bullets.

Tom Wintringham

Granien

Too many people are in love with death
And he walks thigh-proud, never sleeps alone;
Consider him neighbour and enemy, both
Hated and usual, best avoided when
Best known.

Weep, weep, weep! say machine-gun bullets, stating
Mosquito-like a sharper note near by;
Hold steady the torch, the black, the torn flesh lighting,

And the searching probe; carry the stretcher; wait,
Eyes dry.

Our enemies can praise death and adore death;
For us endurance, the sun; and now in this night
The electric torch, feeble, waning, but close-set,
Follows the surgeon's fingers; we are allied with
This light.

David Marshall

I Have Stood To upon Some Lousy Dawns

*At Jarama, Moors crept up behind the sentries guarding the bridge, slit their
throats and mutilated them. The bridge was lost and as a result, many men
were killed.*

I have stood to upon some lousy dawns
When even insects slept
Demanded friend from foe – a silly drill
No army reg. nor proper polished button
Could guard against the dark patrol
The silent knife that slits the gullet
And gushes blood in all our cavities
The fascist pig is rooting in our garden
And many men were cut and cut again,
Their bollocks shoved in broken mouths.
We had not guessed at this atrocity
For Franco chose to use these infidels
To strengthen his most Christian crusade.

Eric Edney

The Battalion Goes Forward

From Chinchón across the Tajuña
Six hundred men set out,
Knowing the odds against them
But harbouring never a doubt,

Towards San Martín went marching,
Crossing the sunken road,
Topping the hills and gazing
Down where the Jarama flowed.

With our Franco-Belgian comrades
We lads took up our posts,
With the Dimitrov, Thaelmann and Spanish
Awaiting the fascist hosts;
Thirty thousand opposing
A handful of untried men ...
What was the chance of holding
The road to Valencia then?

And yet, since we knew the reasons
That had brought us to Spain to fight,
We halted the Moorish legions,
The Italian and German might.
With our second company captured,
With half now for ever still,
The fascists ne'er saw the Tajuña
The other side of the hill.

Then, who vanquished the Spanish people?
Who beat off each fierce attack?
Fascists there are without labels,
And *they* stabbed Spain in the back.
So now we trust not the fair words
Of Daladier and Chamberlain,
When they cry: 'Freedom is in peril!'
We answer: 'Who murdered Spain?'

So this February we remember
Our comrades dead on the ridge,
And swear in our new positions
To hold the Arganda bridge;
With the knowledge that Spain has taught us
To keep open freedom's ways,
And to hold all fascist battalions
As in the Jarama days.

Thomas O'Brien

On Guard for Liberty

Those who have been close
To feel the deed like hot blood flowing
Are apart and silent in the heart of it;
They cannot speak full words –
There are no words to make a living man
Live on again through this,
No words to make one die again
As one has died.
To the blood and bone of future races
This heart will beat,
Children born in the strength of it
Hardly knowing what it is that makes them free
And we close circled by our little fires
Waiting night to take these last few friendly shadows
In a quiet sector of this Spanish war zone
Breathing with these men
Send back messages of faith in the future.

1938

Pat O'Reilly

A Dying Comrade's Farewell to His Sweetheart

You can tell my little sweetheart that I send her all my love.
You can tell her that I love her and in death I love her still.
You can tell her that my body lies where the Jarama river flows,
Where Spanish guns still flash and the Workers' Army goes.

Oh! Well do I remember her farewell kiss to me.
She told me not to falter when the fascist guns did roar
But to show the Spanish workers that we're with them to the last
And to defend their country from Moorish savage hands.

When Franco threw his terror amongst the working class
Our comrades were determined that they'd fight him to the last
For we'd sooner die than see fascism rule this land.
Loud on high we raise the cry, fascism shall not pass.

27 February 1937

John Cornford

To Margot Heinemann

Heart of the heartless world,
Dear heart, the thought of you
Is the pain at my side,
The shadow that chills my view.

The wind rises in the evening,
Reminds that autumn is near.
I am afraid to lose you,
I am afraid of my fear.

On the last mile to Huesca,
The last fence for our pride,
Think so kindly, dear, that I
Sense you at my side.

And if bad luck should lay my strength
Into the shallow grave,
Remember all the good you can;
Don't forget my love.

John Lepper

Battle of Jarama 1937

The sun warmed the valley
But no birds sang
The sky was rent with shrapnel
And metallic clang

Death stalked the olive trees
Picking his men
His leaden finger beckoned
Again and again

Dust rose from the roadside
A stifling cloud

Ambulances tore past
Klaxoning loud

Men torn by shell-shards lay
Still on the ground
The living sought shelter
Not to be found

Holding their hot rifles
Flushed with the fight
Sweat-streaked survivors
Willed for the night

With the coming of darkness
Deep in the wood
A fox howled to heaven
Smelling the blood.

Charles Donnelly

The Tolerance of Crows

Death comes in quantity from solved
Problems on maps, well-ordered dispositions,
Angles of elevation and direction;

Comes innocent from tools children might
Love, retaining under pillows,
Innocently impaled on any flesh.

And with flesh falls apart the mind
That trails thought from the mind that cuts
Thought clearly for a waiting purpose.

Progress of poison in the nerves and
Discipline's collapse is halted.
Body awaits the tolerance of crows.

Ralph Cantor

'Twas postwar stalemate period'

'Twas postwar stalemate period
The workers' power was latent
The needle hovered flashpoint
At fascist bluff so blatant

Imperialism by the press
The radio and crown
Attempted long with guile and cant
To hold the workers down

When toilers saw approaching dawn
Persuasions no avail
The fascists introduced the axe
The baton and the jail

They smote democracy in Spain
Fascism at its worst
The straw had broke the camel's back
The safety valve had burst

And workers came from other lands
To make the first respond
Who else should show their comradeship
The workers' sterling bond

And who should stop the invader
The fascist murder bands
Than those they seek to subjugate
The workers of all lands

And men who reared from day of birth
Who knew but civil life
Laid down their tools and took up arms
To end this bloody strife

They came from Alexandria
From Warsaw and Brooklyn
Berlin, Paris, Budapest
From Glasgow and Dublin

They left the railroad, mine and mill
The factory and the plough
Ex conscriptees and reserve men
Their training served them now

Escaped from concentration camps
Some went direct to Spain
Old IRA and Schutzbund men
Took up the fight again

Long live our ancient Spartacus
Long live the Commune too
Long live the Russian Bolsheviks
We fight again with you

We carry your traditions
Preserved unspat upon
Long live the glorious Spanish race
The heritage lives on

But how to tackle such a task
A babel mass to function
A hundred nationalities
To work in close conjunction

Accomplishing this marvellous feat
The toilers proved their might
They welded like a mighty rod
Decisive in the fight

The fascist international
United all its power
Unleashing all their tentacles
To crush the Spanish flower

They met and took Manchuria
And Abyssinia too
They meet Madrid but meet therein
The fascist Waterloo

And while I write the battle
Has endured a hundred days

History would sure record
So glorious a phase

No burly Nazi's jackboot
Or Blackshirt from Rome
Will enter in our castle
Or invade the Spanish home

And though we lose some of our great
We save a large amount
'Tis men who live make history
The others will not count

The Frente Popular is strong
Our courage now is famous
We shout aloud 'No pasarán'
'Nosotros pasaremos'

And chroniclers of future times
Will not forget our bid
But save us for a glorious page
Defenders of Madrid

For we who fight to live to-day
Are not drops in the ocean
We're the men who change the world
The crux of future motion

And as one writes one's burning thoughts
Beneath the fascists' fire
One's arm which shoots which toils which writes
Will surely never tire

So let us mourn our fallen
Their actions we don't rue
And let us sing a thousand songs
And let us shout 'Salud'

And let us weep a thousand tears
But let us keep our grace
And let us turn another page
And build a freeborn race

Tony Hyndman

Jarama Front

I tried not to see,
But heard his voice.
How brown the earth
And green the trees.
One tree was his.
He could not move.
Wounded all over,
He lay there moaning.

I hardly knew:
I tore his coat
It was easy –
Shrapnel had helped.

But he was dying
And the blanket sagged.
'God bless you, comrades,
He will thank you.'
That was all.
No slogan,
No clenched fist
Except in pain.

Lon Elliott

Jarama

Unrisen dawns had dazzled in your eyes,
Your hearts were hungry for the not yet born.
In agony of thwarted love and wasted life,
Through all long misery, from countries torn
With savage hands, you did not shrink or bend,
But marched on straighter, prouder to the end.

Not blindly, fighting in another's war,
Lured by cheap promises and drugged with drums,

Striking down brothers in the name of lies,
Slaves of the blackest with all senses numbed –
But clear-eyed, bravely, counting all the cost,
Knowing what might be won, what might be lost.

The rifles you will never hold again
In other hands still speak against the night.
Brothers have filled your places in the ranks
Who will remember how you died for right
The day you took those rifles up, defied
The power of ages, and victorious died.

Comrades, sleep now. For all you loved shall be.
You did not seek for death, but finding it –
And such a death – better than shameful life,
Rest now content. A flame of hope is lit.
The flag of freedom floats again unfurled
And all you loved lives richlier in the world.

Alex McDade

Valley of Jarama

There's a valley in Spain called Jarama,
That's a place that we all know so well,
For 'tis there that we wasted our manhood,
And most of our old age as well.

From this valley they tell us we're leaving
But don't hasten to bid us adieu,
For e'en though we make our departure,
We'll be back in an hour or two.

Oh, we're proud of our British Battalion,
And the marathon record it's made.
Please do us this little favour,
And take this last word to Brigade:

'You will never be happy with strangers,
They would not understand you as we.

So remember the Jarama Valley
And the old men who wait patiently.'

Charles Donnelly

Heroic Heart

Ice of heroic heart seals plasmic soil
Where things ludicrously take root
To show in leaf kindnesses time had buried
And cry music under a storm of 'planes,
Making thrust head to slacken, muscle waver
And intent mouth recall old tender tricks.
Ice of heroic heart seals steel-bound brain.

There newer organs built for friendship's grappling
Waste down like wax. There only leafless plants
And earth retain disinterestedness.
Though magnetised to lie of the land, moves
Heartily over the map wrapped in its iron
Storm. Battering the toads, armoured columns
Break walls of stone or bone without receipt.
Jawbones find new way with meats, loins
Raking and blind, new way with women.

Ewart Milne

Thinking of Artolas

Sirs and Señoras, let me tell you a story.
A story neither of long ago nor faraway
But close enough now and to you unhappily.
We will call it Going-Into-History
And you all know History is a cruel country
Where tiger terraces crouch drinking rivers waterless
And sheep immobilised by sombrero shepherds' piping ...
It could be set in Estremadura or Cordova,
Time crawling like inches and napoleonic wars

Dogeared in textbooks seeming the latest in strategy –
At least until recently. Or as Shaw might have said
The life force gets going but man has his lag ...
True. And to gain on his lag must man lose his leg,
And truncate himself, as in Estremadura?

Well, at Casada's we ate ortolans elsewhere we drank coffee.
In the Gran Vía in the Colón we went into conference.
All day the starlings on the Ramblas whispered,
All day the dead air pacified the street,
Fat pigeons swaggered on the Plaza Cataluña.
It was easy enough to analyse an ortolan,
Conjure pigeon into pie: translate con leche ...

But the starlings worried me, and their whispering,
I could never understand their whispering.
It weaved breathlessly up and up like the Coulin –
Or like that dissonance outsoaring ecstasy, heard
Near any roadside or beside any bed, disrupting the
Lovers enlaced, singing with no sound and saying
'O the world is bright and empty.'

At Madrid we dined with the newspaper bunch.
So-and-so shouted they all called him a Fascist –
There *had* been whispers – but he didn't care
He shouted for Empire. That was all right
Empire shouted for him – one supposes, somewhere.
All day I was a method of analysis ... Did my heart, Tomás,
Or your depthless eyes tell me analysis was cowardly
While Los Madrileños were barricading their old Madrid out?
... All day So-and-so the Fascist was blustering.
I analysed his quality as extreme
Scatology and efficiency walking backwards, with a shrug ...
But sadly I knew the whispering starlings
Wintering would rise from the Plaza Cataluña
Before I returned.

With Jarama held they brought him in, the tankist.
From his Georgian hair the blood smiled through,
And smiled on the paving and from the verandah
Smiled as it dripped and adventured below ...
In parks they dream of penny murder non-intervention –

He took the hammered blow and said Salud –
All day my heart with love was helpless, all day I knew
He had gone further than I towards finding a synthesis.
With Jarama held his wound wore on, the Georgian
Who held a dawnstar and not nettles as we do –
Whisper, starlings, whisper! Be incorruptible and saying
'O the world is bright and always living'.

Sirs and Señoras, let me end my story –
I show you earth, earth formally,
And Two on guard with the junipers.
Two, Gael and Jew side by side in a trench
Gripping antique guns to flick at the grasshoppers
That zoomed overhead and the moon was rocking.
Two who came from prisonment, Gael because of Tone,
Jew because of human love, the same for Jew as German –
Frail fragments both, chipped off and forgotten readily ...

I set them together, Izzy Kupchik and Donnelly;
And of that date with death among the junipers
I say only, they kept it: and record the exploded
Spreadeagled mass when the moon was later
Watching the wine that baked earth was drinking.
Such my story, Sirs and Señoras. Whether you like it
Or pay a visit to your vomitorium, is all one ...
Perhaps you'll like the junipers and a moon steadied,
High baked earth and night's formalism,
Remembering that History is always a cruel country
And crueller man than April.

Laurie Lee

A Moment of War

> It is night like a red rag
> drawn across the eyes
>
> the flesh is bitterly pinned
> to desperate vigilance
>
> the blood is stuttering with fear.

O praise the security of worms
in cool crumbs of soil,
flatter the hidden sap
and the lost unfertilized spawn of fish!

The hands melt with weakness
into the gun's hot iron

the body melts with pity,

the face is braced for wounds
the odour and the kiss of final pain.

O envy the peace of women
giving birth and love like toys
into the hands of men!

The mouth chatters with pale curses

the bowels struggle like a nest of rats

the feet wish they were grass
spaced quietly.

O Christ and Mother!

But darkness opens like a knife for you
and you are marked down by your pulsing brain

and isolated

and your breathing,

your breathing is the blast, the bullet,
and the final sky.

Spanish Frontier, 1937

Bill Feeley

Who Wants War?

The landowner spoke: 'When your country's in peril don't fail.'
The lice-cracking soldier views sickly his bloody thumb-nail.
'We've got to have markets,' the rich manufacturer said.
So fatherless children grow pale, lacking sugar and bread.
'Those rapers and looters destroy,' cried the maker of bombs.
From cellars come women to weep by the ruins of homes.

Anonymous

'Munitions men'

Munitions men
Exult again
And say 'What could be finer
With Spain at war
And – what is more –
Japan invading China.'

Bill Harrington

Aragon Ballad

Francisco Franco, fascist chief,
Of him is the story told,
His 'justice' fills the Aragon hills,
His curse is manifold:
He's taken toll of the North and South
The gore it reacheth far;
And they tell the tale of his 'charity'
In the ring at Badajoz.

Francisco Franco, fascist chief,
Of the North and South is told:
That the North and South shall open their mouth

To a People's flag unrolled:
When the big guns speak to an Aragon peak
And his foreign confreres flee –
Ye have heard the song 'How long? How long?'
How long to your victory?

John Dunlop

Brunete, 12 July 1937: An Ode to My Comrades

Beside the road a Yanqui youth
Lies on a stretcher
Body twisting in torment
Shot through with bursts of machine gun fire

The sanitarios strive tenderly
To staunch his pain

I stand there
Looking at him

Every cell in my body on full charge
Desperately trying to pass healing currents
From my strength to his

I cannot stay beside him for the battle calls me
To my own meeting in the morning of life

Soon steel pods of death fly through the skies
Pregnant with deadly seed
Bursting around me on the ground
In instant fatal flowers
Blossoming life away from my comrades, Irish,
French and Scot, Yanqui, German, Spaniard, Slav, Finn and Rus
Greek, Welsh and English, Arab, Jew and Turk,
Black man, Red man, Paleface
We were all there

Stricken I lie with the legs of my comrade stretched over mine
His face a motionless grey mask

The Frenchman still squats, back comfortable against the bank of earth
Speaking not a word
His head has vanished and some blood messes his collar.

Thirty-eight years later I returned to them
Where they lay still and still, forgotten
Under the soil and the sun
Where my blood mingled with theirs
And with their bones fed the dry pale grasses
And small bushes through the years

Like a Mexican warrior of old
I broke off one of the plants
Chewing the stem and swallowing the bitter juice

Then the gods of war and hate
Roared at us once more
With rolls of thunder
Crashing from the battlements of the sky
But all that fell were token tears of gentle drops
To moisten and mingle with my own dry ones

My comrades lie there on a hillside
Forgotten by all but me
With no memorial but dry pale grasses
And small bushes

But now I have raised a monument to them
More lasting than bronze
And higher than the pyramid

This is it.

Miles Tomalin

Wings Overhead

Over Brunete came the sound
Of black wings crawling up the sky;
The soldier crouched against the ground

With straining limbs till they went by.
He heard the bombs sing down the air,
He felt them land, and everywhere
The earth in advancing line
Rose up. The soldier said 'This time'.
This time he laughed at what he said,
And stretched his body to the heat;
The sun alone was overhead
And warmed the terror out of it.

Now, when the thin December gleam
Is driven off the sky by snow
And breath hangs in the air like steam,
The soldier on the plain below
Hears the familiar song of hate
And stoops behind the parapet.
When the black wings have passed beyond
He pulls his blanket closer round,
Grins at the younger man, who tries
To catch his courage from his eyes.
'We'll bring them all down bye and bye,
And then,' he says, 'they'll never come'.
The young man, looking at the sky,
Sees only white wings of the storm.

James R Jump

Sun over the Front

The sun adds to our plight
as we lie face down on the angry earth.
We sweat and, like misers,
conserve our dwindling supply of water,
by now sickly warm.
We shall receive no more before night.
Deliriously I dream of floating away. I dream
of cool sea breezes. I dream
of stretching in tall grass in sycamore shade. I dream
of lying in a fast-flowing mountain stream.
In the sun's face of incandescent brass

there is no smile of compassion.
His hot breath rustles the dry grass
and brings to our line
the scent of pine,
broom and mountain thyme.
The sun smiles no pity on the wounded
out there is no-man's land.
An invisible curtain of potential bullets
hangs between them and us.
Enemy guns warn off
our stretcher-bearers but do not ward off
the sun's vibrant stare.
Our comrades' groans
and pleas for help come to us
on the warm air.
'Oh, madre mía! Madre mía!' one moans.
'Water, water!' another groans.

At last the sun dries
the moisture on their tongues
and evaporates their cries.
By my side
a young Spanish conscript crosses himself,
his lips moving rapidly
without a sound.

Now the suffocating silence is frightening.
We try to forget our friends out there.
We make ourselves concentrate on our own plight
as we lie, face down on the angry earth.
We force ourselves to think of our fight
against the sun.

Tom Wintringham

Poem in the Summer of 1937

Moving across the field a girl in a pink dress,
Over the sky white clouds shadowed with pink,
Dark on my vision, near to me, your black hair;
While the viola and the voice keep

Their lovely argument.
In my hand the spray of elder golden pale
And sweet with summer.

Hay in the meadow cream-folded lies
To darken in the sun, tomorrow and tomorrow,
Richening the scent already heavy
In honey loops on the cream taste of summer.
Feasting goes on all day, all night; all senses
Banquet in June, and love uninterrupted
And tireless wakes in morning, sleeps all night,
Rises and sets in the clear skies of joy.

Not uninterrupted. Love is not
Timeless. Love is over
For thousands who went out this summer weather
And found the feast set, and the feast was death.

And these were ours who died.
Dark on my vision your black hair,
So near to me, it shadows all the sun.

August 1937

Aileen Palmer

Thaelmann Battalion

This is our moment.
You can hear us singing
Where the earth is brittle under the southern sun
Watch us marching in serried ranks to the death that is our homage
To the unbroken spirit of our dishonoured country.

For here we are showing the world our country's other face,
And the voice that for three years in Germany has been silenced
Utters its songs of freedom under an alien sun.

We were in Barcelona with the masses that stormed the Colón;
We left with the first militia for the Eastern Front;
Then we went to Madrid;

We were at Casa de Campo,
Guadalajara, Brunete, Belchite and Teruel,
Putting to rout the Italians in the name of Thaelmann.

Here we have shown to the world our country's other face;
And not the face of the hangman with the sprouting forelock
But the face of the young men who march together singing
Through southern plains where the clay is brittle under the sun.

Sylvia Townsend Warner

Benicasim

Here for a little we pause.
The air is heavy with sun and salt and colour.
On palm and lemon-tree, on cactus and oleander
a dust of dust and salt and pollen lies.
And the bright villas
sit in a row like perched macaws,
and rigid and immediate yonder
the mountains rise.

And it seems to me we have come
into a bright-painted landscape of Acheron.
For along the, strand
in bleached cotton pyjamas, on rope-soled tread,
wander the risen-from-the-dead,
the wounded, the maimed, the halt.
Or they lay bare their hazarded flesh to the salt
air, the recaptured sun,
or bathe in the tideless sea, or sit fingering the sand.

But narrow is this place, narrow is this space
of garlanded sun and leisure and colour, of return
to life and release from living. Turn
(Turn not!) sight inland:
there, rigid as death and unforgiving, stand
the mountains – and close at hand.

Note: At Benicasim on the east coast of Spain is the Rest Home for the conva-
lescent wounded of the Spanish People's Army, and the Villa dedicated to
Ralph Fox, supported by the Spanish Medical Aid.

Norman Brookfield

'Rest, I will know your all-pervading calm'

Rest, I will know your all-pervading calm
Relax my limbs, and feel your soothing balm;
Beneath light's tranquil stars I'll sleep at ease
When dawn's well past, to rise, and day-time fill
With pleasant strolls and food and talk at will.
Shaping vague thoughts beneath the olive trees;
Watching tobacco wreathe its lazy fumes
Quintessence rare, o rest of your perfumes.
And yet this is a respite that must end
An interval between the course of war
Which all too soon will raise its dreadful roar,
Bidding my laggard pace once more to mend;
But 'tis the thoughts of past and future strife
That make you sweet, O rest, and with you – life.

1938, Spain

Miles Tomalin

Lull in War

The sound of an accordian

Even this music raises its head to an imaginary sky
Like trees on a hill,
Like the bright striped scarf round the gypsy's hair:
These coarsely cut strong chords
Throw colour in swift shafts into the war-time night,
Bringing over darkness a momentary sun,
They are as warm as a wide fire burning in a grate,
Making the room too hot,
Stirring the blood roughly like crude red Spanish wine.

James R Jump

Ebro Crossing

Soon we shall launch the attack.
This is no routine manoeuvre.
We must regain
the ground we lost three months back.

All my belongings have gone in a lorry
to the safety of the rear
and I am alone,
wearing my tattered uniform and my fear.
In my pockets I have nothing of my own –
not even a pocket-knife or comb.
I have no money and not a single photograph
to transport me, temporarily
from the war.
I have a 1908 rifle,
fifty cartridges stuffed in my pockets
and two hand-grenades tied to my belt.
In my blanket-roll I have a loaf of bread
and a tin of corned beef.
My tin mug and water-bottle are securely tied
so that they will not rattle when I run,
crouching,
in my rope-soled sandals
or crawl on my belly
like an ungainly tailless lizard.

If I am lucky and come out of the front line
in, maybe, ten days' time,
I shall have my own things again –
a book of Lorca poems,
a badge in the colours of Republican Spain,
Cayetana's photograph,
a fountain-pen and a change of socks.

But first, we have to launch the attack.

Miles Tomalin

Down the Road

My letter reached the girl on holiday,
She read it walking down a seaside lane
And felt, instead of me being far away
She walked with me in Spain.

Next walk I took, I fancied she was there,
'You don't hear birds,' I said. 'You may hear shells.
The one that misses us hits someone else,
And now and then it hits him fair and square.

'There's one beside the highway further on,
I saw it happen, and got a cursing too,
Because I told his pal the man was through.

There wasn't anything he could have done.
Why, the man's blood was thickening on the ground,
The grey had reached his face, and when he spoke
There wasn't any sound.

'Death on an English country road seems huge,
One sight would spoil your holiday,' I said.
'But here one doesn't let one's feelings loose
Even when a man one knew and liked is dead.

'One murder, and all England makes a fuss;
God knows, one cigarette means more to us.
War's crude, oh sure.
But you can tell the smug ones over there
Another hair's breadth, it'll be the same
To walk in England as to walk in Spain.'

Written in Spain, 1938

Tony McLean

Full Moon over Barcelona, 1938

They called you virgin
though you stooped down to kiss your bumpkin lover
on such a night.
They called you chaste
though the infatuate greenhorn sighed his soul
drenched with your light.

Peroxide spy
your spider fingers intimately seek
reveal our city
smirk at your Junkers
and kiss your darling Fiats, where peoples groan
bombed without pity.

Bill Harrington

To a Fallen Comrade

With those that bled, with those that gave their lives,
Who had no thought for individual gain,
But rather, as a man, like one who strives
For fellow men, he joined the fight in Spain.

He fought to aid a people, strong and great,
Forged in steel, by common struggle one;
Fought to see a world that knew not hate –
That all might take a place beneath the sun.

He will not see the people that shall rise
In the new-born world for which he gave his life;
Yet o'er his grave, a sound that never dies –
A happier, joyous sound, unmarred by strife.

Thomas O'Brien

International Brigade Dead

A lonely student in a silent room
Quits his lagging pen to dream
Of thundering mountains;
Crouches, tight-faced, where the vine-stump
Spreads its silent singing leaves,
Still eyes where the lifting dust
Speaks of death;
Leaps from vine to covering vine
To the mound of safety;
Dies, as fancy has it,
Gladly on the sun's bright theatre.

An old man lifts his misty eye
To the brown ceiling of his life,
Regrets the nearness of his papered walls,
Wonders why he dared not dare
The sun to cast his leaning shadow
Forward on a page of time
Unticked by clocks on tidy mantels.

A poet takes the sudden bayonet gleam to paper,
Waking hurried echoes in the huddled hills,
Not for any prideful lust or wing-clipped cause –
But for their beauty, those children of the wonder-moment,
Who dared to die in youth that youth might live.

Where the rising sun is,
Where the setting sun is,
Where the wind is
And the rain,
Where the striding spirit is
They go in their battalions,
Eager as the elements they conquered.

With you, O youth, forever,
They shall never rest in peace.

1939

Miles Tomalin

To England from the English Dead

We, who were English once had eyes and saw
The savage greed of those who made this war
Tear up from earth, like a hog loose in flowers
So many lives as young and strong as ours,
You, England, stood apart from Spain's affair
You said you were secure in sea and cliff
While others sank in filthy war, as if
You kept some old virginity in there.
While the black armies marched and the dead fell,
You toldeo [sic] your English people all was well,
And shutting eyes to war was finding peace.
You told them once, all slavery must cease.
Dishonourable England! We in Spain
Who died, died proudly, but not in your name;
Our friends will keep the love we felt for you
Among your maist [sic] green landscapes and smooth hills,
Talk of it over honest window sills,
And teach our children we were not untrue.
Not for those others, more like alien men
Who, quick to please our slayers, let them pass,
Not for them
We English lie beneath the Spanish grass.

Clive Branson

England

I thought England green with pleasant valleys
dividing smooth fields rich to stroke
to lie with one's face sideways in the grass
watching a stretch of trembling water;

From doors of dark and grimy alleys
in huge spreading cities, breathing smoke,
through black cracks in curtained windows
pale houses queer.

I thought England safe where the brook
broke silence over the pebbles, where the rows
of houses parallel to the sky over the hill
where the white clouds, smoke, look
to see what we're doing, asking
'Help the people of Spain'.

From the valleys grey with dust
from the hopeless homes of people
from the alleys long forgotten
by the scum who fight against us
by the rich who starve the people
from ragged clothes and dirty pockets
sewn and cleaned a thousand times
comes the will to pay the price
comes the penny's mighty sacrifice
comes the warmth of friendliness.

England's subdued voices tell
how Freedom strode inside the closed forest of Sherwood.
Breath of England!
How men marched from North and South and East and West on
London.
Heart of England!
How they would mould it all
and name it after them
England.

February 1939

Lorenzo Varela (translated by Lon Elliott)

Spain, May 1st, 1938

1
There is no rest or peace in all this land,
Along this bitter, this hard-trodden road,
And in these hearts.
Listen, road-menders, shepherds,
Workers of Paris, London and the world
There is no rest or peace in all this land!

2
Men, workers like yourselves, they too
With bullocks yoked to plough just like your own,
With lathes like yours,
Or dusty flocks smelling of rosemary,
Under the same sky, in the same factories,
Trudging and working, and never resting.

3
Men, workers like yourselves, they too
With children just as lovely
And sheets as poor on beds just like your own,
And with fresh bread that smells as good as yours,
Fight on and triumph under olive trees
And in the yellow cornfields,
And on the eternal snow that sleeps beneath the pines.

4
Under a manly sky, men among men,
Strong and glad as you are strong and glad,
Leave in forgetfulness
Their blazing houses and their old folk crippled.
There is no rest or peace in all this land
Which shall forever bear the name of Spain! –
Because we are and shall be the only masters of the day,
Masters of all our cities, and the real masters of our fields.

5
The men from the mines,
The herdsmen and the men from up the hills,
The men who make the bread and those who grow the wheat,
The poets, blacksmiths, woodworkers,
Defending here a people's name and life
On the baked soil out with advance posts,
And in the factories.

6
There is no rest or peace in all this land!
But only flowers growing in earthen pots.
Letters the Artillery finished.
And men who do not rest,
Are ever watchful, like our chestnut trees,
And stand on guard, waiting for victory's fruits.

James R Jump

Shared Cigarette

Half a century ago,
during a brief lull in the battle,
we shared a cigarette –
the last of ten Woodbines
sent to me in a rolled-up newspaper.
With it we made
two skeleton-thin smokes
and sighed contentedly
as we inhaled,
filling our lungs with sweet harshness.
Later that day, you were killed
and we buried your body there
on the mountain facing Gandesa.

Fifty years later
you still meander
along the margins of my mind,
making sudden incursions
into the misty memory.
Without warning, your face appears
and I see again the ever-present grin,
the twinkling eyes,
the stubbled chin.

Then I recall how you looked
slumped over your now silenced machinegun.
In your shirt pocket we found
an empty pouch –
not a fibre, not a crumb of tobacco in it.
I was glad then,
and still am,
that I shared with you, George,
my last Woodbine

12 July 1988

Bill Harrington

Farewell

The barren soil grows rich
With Life's red blood,
And fertile peace shall hide
This black terrain;
Youth and joy shall thunder
As in flood,
To drown the dust of war
The weeds of pain.
And as the sun comes up
And reddened skies
Reflect the glory of
The sacrificed:
A thousand voices shall
In echo rise,
To greet this new-born land
In vict'ry's tryst.

Anonymous

Eyes

Eyes of men running, falling, screaming
Eyes of men shouting, sweating, bleeding
The eyes of the fearful, those of the sad
The eyes of exhaustion, and those of the mad.

Eyes of men thinking, hoping, waiting
Eyes of men loving, cursing, hating
The eyes of the wounded sodden in red
The eyes of the dying and those of the dead.

Ewart Milne

Song of the Night Market

Through the silent squares
The guitar tinkles loud.

    Do you remember Carlos, María?
    His kindling song
    To the balustrade rising,
    On the dubious calm
    Of the evening.
    Do you remember Carlos, María,
    Now the grandees are back in the castles?

    Dust is his death, María.
    His poet's blood rusts
    The spades of labourers,
    Bending their backs
    In the fields of olive.
    Do you remember Carlos, María,
    Now the grandees are back in the castles?

The guitar tinkles loud
Through the silent squares.

Clive Branson

The Nightingale

You spent your voice upon the midnight air
Here, when we were newcomers, you were alone.
No one listened. Your music died to share
Each tedious darkness with the deaf mute moon.

A sleepless captive swears to hear you sing
Whom his sorrow renders still. We too cower
Awake under the dead blanket thinking
Of that illusive freedom you echo each hour

And even through the shouting of the guard
Their chain of noise, we hear you secret bird,
Their strength, their arrogance, though bayonet proud
Can't still the voice humanity has heard.

Your silence is articulate when you
Must be obedient, sing when ordered to.

San Pedro, 1938

Clive Branson

San Pedro

A foreign darkness fills the air to-night.
The moon betrays this unfamiliar scene.
Strange creatures, shadow-ghosts of what had been
Live with no aim than groping through half-light,
Talk dreamily, walk wandering, delight
In trivial acts that formerly would mean
Nothing. A livid memory, this lean
Ill-clad rabble of a lost dreaded might.

Look longer, deeper, the accustomed eyes
Know more than quick appearances can tell.
These fools, this shoddy crowd, this dirt, are lies
Their idiot captors wantonly compel.
These men are giants chained down from the skies
To congregate an old and empty hell.

Aileen Palmer

'The dead have no regrets'

The dead have no regrets: they went
Proudly to their tumultuous doom.
But, sitting in a crowded room,
We mourn our lives too tamely spent.

We shut the door and turn the lock,
But, while we talk and analyse,
Within our ears, before our eyes,
Ticks the implacable clock.

To-day we gather up the threads,
Discuss the issue, great or small;
Perhaps to-morrow it will fall –
The Sword that hangs above our heads.

Black wings are massed against the dawn.
What will it matter that we rhyme
Our Chronicles of Wasted Time
If liberty is gone?

What will it matter that we write
Our own Remembrance of Things Past,
If all we write can only last
Until to-morrow night?

If all the books from which we learn,
The poets that we praise to-day,
Before the onslaught of decay
With Lorca and Heine burn,

If Europe's walls come tumbling down
(And one by one the bastions fall)
What will it matter if we all
In that great chaos drown?

We search the minutes we have spent,
But feel in Time's relentless beat
The threat of ultimate defeat.
Only the dead can rest content,

Having given all they had to give,
To save from blood and fire and dust
At least a hope that we can trust.
We must remember them – and live.

London 1939

David Marshall

Retrospect

Go back –
Six feet of snow on the Aragon front;
While here
Kids slide in the roadways
Steadied feet thudding in the gutters:
Ice blurs
The red orange blue of neon lights –
The harlot shops invite.
But there
The café lights blink and blacken
Ribs tighten, skin grows ware –
After the momentary adjustment
A fumbling for the tasteless glass –
A startled touch of warm-whorled fingers
A greedy intake of smoke
– The lung-shock battens the nerves –
Strange faces glow intimate
Red-arc'd by the fitful cigarette.

Distant shots
Snap at lit windows –
Tenseness strangles the blood –
The walls reverberate
From an anti-aircraft in the church next door
That coughs dully, cough, cough …

Vienen los aviones, ay ay,
Los aviones, says some woman –
Carven deu, tancat la boca …
Then the bombs
Belching earth-pits
Quagging the ground,
One two three sudden,
Four, wait wait wait five,
Six god that's it
Shattering, rumbling racket
Glass smashing and one thin endless scream.
Then a dullness in the head,

We stand over the table,
A glass falls, rings,
The air tastes of the Metro.
The cigarettes are all out.
A no-sex voice from the street
Cries Sanidad Sanidad
– Christ let's get out of this ...
Ay, allí mucha de la muerte hay,
Y aquí, qué hay mejor.

Ewart Milne

The Hour Glass (1)

Dryly across the street the late leaves fall Barcelona falls.
From the mind as from a wall the map of Spain stares squarely
And like the leaves in silence is not to be evaded.
How often and dumbly I revisit that city those provinces,
Salute again the outposts see again the mules meander up and
    slowly
Wind along the grey road to Cuenca to the parched plateau ...
And your voice merging with memory is lost in the lost provinces
Where that army marched was cold and died and women from their
    empty shops came stumbling –
Ah now, I whisper, where now is the sanctuary! –
Then as your voice reassures me urgently then still
The olives broken by the sands and sea
Slope down and mean whatever they meant when I saw them
Bearing their wounds like a gain or a bud of reckoning.

Hearing your voice
Strange and urgent and as if through eddying
Nowhere tides of people stumbling, through the siege of cities,
I am conscious of that quality inescapable
In falling leaves of leaves in secret budding,
Clad O in all winter's harness
This glimpse comes brightening.

Clive Branson

On the Statue of the Virgin
which stood as a pair with that of Christ, at Palencia. It was bombed
and destroyed early on in the war.

Another statue – has since disappeared –
once crowned a sister hill – a monstrous thing!
When girls twine flowers round their heads in Spring
death took the Virgin our religion feared.

When from the skies new wings the statue neared
to rout Spain's enemies from their hiding
in a black priest's gown, the Virgin's clothing;
the monument was smashed, the sky-line cleared.

The sculptor is not dead – bone white, dust white,
he carves again though blood is on his hand
staining the new marble, day-break and night.

When life ran through their fingers like white sand
the workman built a school for his delight;
the peasant bent and rested on his land.

2 June 1939

Anonymous

Salud, Brigade – Salud!

In days unborn, when tales are told
Of Freedom's vanguard, strong and bold,
When o'er the world a hush is spread,
And we pay homage to our dead,
A cry will ring in every heart:
    Salud! Brigade, Salud!

They, in our hearts, will never die,
Who carried Freedom's banner high,
And fighting died, and gave their all
To break the strangling Fascist thrall.
That cry must live for ever:
    Salud! Brigade, Salud!

We, who are young, must all unite,
A deeper fire yet we'll light,
To show the path that we must tread,
If we with honour face our dead.
They will answer in response:
    Salud! Comrades, Salud!

David Marshall

I Sing of My Comrades

I sing of my comrades
That once did sing the Internationale
In that great choir at Albacete
Before the battle. Rank after rank
Of the young battalions
Singing the Internationale
They came from every corner of the earth
So many men from distant lands
Who took to arms in the defence
Of Spain's Republic.

Madrid the magnet that drew us all
Along slow roads to Spain – at last a star
For desperate men, sensing the gathering storm
And we that fought to warn a watching world
Were called false prophets by appeasers
Yet we fought for the poor of the world.

Our lullabies were soldiers' songs
Sung by sad women to the sons of the fallen.
And remembered in Remembrance Day long past
After the thudding drum and shriek of bugles
I listened to the slow lament
For brothers, sons and lovers lost.
It is the sadness in the singing,
The undertones of woe,
The deep vein of grief
That throbs throughout my generation.

Tony McLean

'I wept the day that Barcelona fell'

I wept the day that Barcelona fell
and who would fear such honest tears to own?
Who when such spheres collided would not groan?
And you who wept not, yes, I hate you well
ignoble English bound with Munich spell
where moral climate could not move to shame
what shall it profit if I sum your blame
now London's suffered passiontide as well?
Yet Spain's still bound, three times the cock did crow,
that would not bend her knee; no Malchus swords
came to her aid, no midwife time affords
to ease the childpangs she must undergo.
Christopher lost, John gone and Edward slain
while you hugged safety and abandoned Spain.

Bill Harrington

In an Olive Grove

I wandered thro' the tortured grove
Where 'midst the ruined trees we drove
The fiends of war to final death;
That they might give to you and me
Heritage of a world set free.
And there beneath a twisted limb,
Beneath whose scars life crossed the brim;
There beside a riven stem
Alone which marks the grave of men
Who gave their lives to see unfurled
The standard of Man in a better world
There I sat and the vision rose,
A glorious galaxy of those
Whose youth and hopes were sacrificed
To dreams they had of paradise
To brave ideals of a virtuous earth
Their years were shed to bring the birth

Of a boundless joy that will amply repay
The everything that they gave away.

David Martin

Remember

You shall sing their song, their proud song again,
You shall sing this soldierly song!
Of Arganda Bridge and the Ebro campaign,
Of those of us who were buried in Spain,
And of hearts that beat bravely and strong.

Remember Jarama? The poppies lay red
Where we broke the Moorish assault.
We came many men strong and left many men dead,
And many a brave British working class lad
Fought Junkers with rifle and colt.

Remember Arganda? Remember the fight
For Las Rozas and Carabanchel?
Remember Brunete? The night was bright
With burning woods and a village alight,
At Brunete, where Nathan fell.

Remember, remember – a comrade, a name,
A white house, a river, a hill,
A name of glory, of hatred or fame;
We came from afar, but we knew why we came,
And we knew how to die and to kill.

Remember us brother in mill and in plant,
You miner, you sailor, all you
Comrades who built by the might of your hand
Fair ships and great cities; last heirs of this land,
Forget not the best of your crew.

You shall sing their song, their proud song again,
You shall sing this soldierly song!
When we fight in England's last campaign.
You shall sing of the lads we have buried in Spain,
And of hearts that beat bravely and strong.

Tony McLean

For Antonio Tessaro of Padua, Missing in Aragon, 1938

Where Giambettino mixed his burning paints
and harsh Mantegna with astringent style
painted renascent Christs that dare not smile
Roman Madonnas and metallic saints
there, there I say from that Venetian plain
Paduan Antonio innocent of guile
jesting with buoyant heart at all denial
anonymous and joyful came to Spain.
Who would have guessed that in that carefree vein
Mantegna's secret steel lay hid so deep
as pregnant girls their strange contentment keep
fulfilled with hope and undismayed by pain?
Fallen in Spain, your seed rich harvest yields
where partisans bloom in the Italian fields.

Jim Haughey

Fighter Pilot

I think that it will come, somewhen, somewhere
In shattering crash, or roaring sheet of flame;
In the green-blanket sea, choking for air,
Amid the bubbles transient as my name.

Sometimes a second's throw decides the game,
Winner takes all, and there is no re-play,
Indifferent earth and sky breathe on the same,
I scatter my last chips, and go my way.

The years I might have had I throw away:
They only lead to winter's barren pain.
Their loss must bring no tears from those who stay,
For Spring, however spent, comes not again.

When peace descends once more like gentle rain,
Mention my name in passing, if you must,
As one who knew the terms – slay or be slain,
And thought the bargain was both good and just.

Anonymous

For Spain and for Sam Wild

Now – remember the heart.
Not much is known of it,
For so the heart is and was ever, not much known about.
Write … of little water-drops making a river
And the river subterrene, the fuller for the damming.
Write … of revolt and revenge, and waiting,
Of planning and the sporadic coup de main on the mountain,
Truck-train of munitions, for Germany, blown up,
The anonymous deed, here and there, its import a very hinge
But the event furled into itself, the cosecha later
When whatever year it be orders the harvest.
Write of the heart – they'll understand you, the Spaniards will.

This land
Is a palimpsest – is it not –
Scored over and over with pain,
And with strength furrowed, and hammered with endeavour.
An example
Of how waiting tempers the coming sword.
Here nothing is lost – no vagueness, no compromise
In the plain straight line of things
As they should be – and will be.

Numantium –
That pain is gone, passed into time's earth
With Cervantes to fight it again. (Oh Father Ebro,
And a skull-full of Romans, and the Numantian fury.)
Done, it is over. BC150. But the temper of it's left:
Resistance, death: palimpsest. Spain is guerilla.
Into the hills gone, where no guardia dare follow,
Nature and man – rock and Spain – as ever united here.
Not the crafty Nazi,
Nor the mechanised hysteria of machines
Reduces. And if the iron rain came again?
You cannot put out a volcano with dynamite.

You will want to look back on that war – see it as a ridge
Blocking capture – without arms much – very high,

And the city of Madrid, the heart, the fortaleza,
Wall of the world, rampart against the Fascist tide.
See it as hunger and the unheated room
With the Castilian wind through the winter shell-hole there,
The drawn thin face, the gaunt crazy meal,
Sandbags and cold – the bean in all its nakedness.
   Battle without weapon
   Battle with starvation
   Battle against treachery –
   Now, battle of writing.

It is not necessary, as elsewhere it *is* necessary
To bowl the message along: 'The country will rise again';
They need no trumpets they whose being is the whole of this.

We're a long way from all of that here now ...
And then, a pair of eyes burning burning in a pub one night,
Led the British in the IBs then – yes, time is a train
Our train, and we know it Sam, will conquer the longest track ...
A long long way from the inspiration here now
This London '42's October, yet here is the brand,
You, travelling fire, camarada – I've named you, Sam Wild.

David Martin

Jarama

Children unborn then have forgotten their dolls now.
The small green olive trees are no longer small.
White House over Morata! Twice chalk has healed over
Bullet scars traced into shutter and wall.

The Bishop was hard then, he is feeble and cold now;
His vintner was eager, now the devil is beckoning.
But longer than time dreams Sancho the peasant,
Stronger than trees and the stranger's strange reckoning.

See: Many nations have put on spring's joy robe,
She is still shrouded in black of her slavery
And the night of her eyes is dark in the morning,
Mourning her sons, red tears for their bravery.

We said we will return to the house by the crossroads,
From the corners of the earth we shall come again.
Years shall not master us, we will master them.
We said: He is waiting. We will come back to Spain.

Add horror to terror, add fighting to waiting,
Add manhood to childhood, add singing to weeping;
O hills of Jarama, White House over Morata!
We have said that the hour will not find us sleeping.

Bert Neville

England, Arise

England, stately England,
How can you tranquil be?
India's ravished land
Still groans in slavery.

Cruel famine stalks her land;
Oh, where your lofty pride?
England – Oh my England,
Lie not with Death as Bride.

In the war-torn countries
Vile traitors still go free –
In France – in Spain and Greece
Your guilt is plain to see.

Oh set my conscience free
And cleanse this stain, I crave;
Must England ever be
The gaoler of the brave?

Now let the slaves go free!
Dear land that gave me birth;
Thus shall your greatness be
Acclaimed throughout the Earth.

August, 1945

Aileen Palmer

Letter from the Underworld

For the English

Me lords and ladies, you'll forget,
no doubt, that we have ever met,

Or may think, with a spasm of pain,
'One of the crowd I knew in Spain ...'

Our underworld is different now:
folk live in affluence, and how!

Old boys get knighthoods, and they get Thistles:
with aristocracy it bristles,

But, lords and ladies, don't forget
somewhere on Freedom Road we met ...

Caliban

Tony McLean

'Have we no Dante for to-day's Aquinas?'

Have we no Dante for to-day's Aquinas?
Read our dull novels and ill-written tracts
angular style and careless of their facts
small wonder that the critics still malign us
to their waste-paper baskets soon consign us.
O for a tongue to tell Spain's tragedy.
O Spartacus in torment on the tree
arise and shine and with your blood refine us.
O for a voice to sing that toilsome fight
bull-ring at Badajoz's mad butchery
the battle-cruisers belching their cruelty
at Málaga's mother and child in flight.
Blackbird most royal, by the sharp falcon slain
rise from the dark, inspire resurgent Spain.

Miles Tomalin

Aftermath

The conferring of the Freedom of Guernica on Generalissimo Francisco Franco

Through the undisputed heaven,
Bent on hopes of greater glories
Than the battle fronts had given
Came the fascist trimotores,
On Guernica loosed their venom,
Hammered helpless men and women
Into pulped and writhing earth.
Thus they brought the blitz to birth.

Gaudily across the passes
Now no longer barricaded,
White hope of the ruling classes
Since all other hopes have faded,
Franco rides with pomp and pageant,
Little salesman, foreign agent,
Rides between the flags and vistas
Staged by anxious falangistas
To receive the freedom ordered
From the city that he murdered.

Eyes in all the darker places,
Round the door, behind the pillar,
Eyes gleam from hidden faces,
Eyes are levelled at the killer.
Fear of what's to come is stirring,
Tyrants' deaths are squalid, gory,
Mussolini, Hitler, Goering
Left him to complete the story.
Here, in eyes that have no pity
He may read the final chapter:
Thus within the murdered city
Freedom waits to greet her captor.

Scorched and splintered lie its stones,
Blood is dust with flesh and hair,
Whiter runs the street for bones –

El Caudillo's welcome there.
There the friendly maggot fêtes him
With his pomp and pinchbeck fasces,
There the city's freedom waits him
Where he left its dust and ashes.

Tom Wintringham

Monument

When from the deep sky
And digging in the harsh earth,
When by words hard as bullets,
Thoughts simple as death,
You have won victory,
People of Spain,
You will remember the free men who fought beside you, enduring
and dying with you, the strangers
Whose breath was your breath.

You will pile into the deep sky
A tower of dried earth,
Rough as the walls where bullets
Splashed men to death
Before you won victory,
Before you freed Spain
From the eating gangrene of wealth, the grey pus of pride, the black
scab of those strangers
Who were choking your breath.

Bring together, under the deep sky
Metal and earth;
Metal from which you made bullets
And weapons against death,
And earth in which, for victory,
Across all Spain,
Your blood and ours was mingled, Huesca to Málaga; earth to which
your sons and strangers
Gave up the same breath.

Bring to the tower, to its building,
From New Castile,
From Madrid, the indomitable breast-work,
Earth of a flower-bed in the Casa de Campo,
Shell-splinters from University City,
Shell-casing from the Telefónica.
Bring from Old Castile, Santander, Segovia,
Sandbags of earth dug out of our parapets
And a false coin stamped in Burgos by a traitor.

Carry from León, from the province of Salamanca,
Where the bulls are brave and the retired generals cowards,
From near the Capital of treason and defeat, bring now
Clean earth, new and untouched, from the cold hills,
And iron from the gate, that shall now be always open
Of Spain's oldest school, where there shall be young wisdom.

From Extremadura, earth from the bullring
Where they shot the prisoners in Badajoz;
And lovely Zafra shall give one of its silver crosses;
Galicia, sea-sand and ship-rivets. From Asturias
Spoil from the pits that taught our dynamiters
To face and destroy the rearing tanks, and a pit-haft
That has cut coal and trenches, and is still fit for work.
From the Basque country, Bilbao, Guernica,
City of agony, villages of fire,
Take charred earth, so burnt and tortured no one
Knows if small children's bones are mingled in it;
Take iron ore from the mines those strangers envied;
And wash your hands, remembering a world that did so.

Navarre shall give a ploughshare and a rock;
Aragon, soil from the trench by the walnut-tree
Where Thaelmann's first group fought towards Huesca,
And steel from a wrecked car lying by a roadside;
Lukacsz rode in that car.
Catalonia; Spain and not Spain, and our gateway
(For myself a gateway to Spain and courage and love)
Shall bring a crankshaft from the Hispano factory
And earth from Durrutti's grave;
Valencia, black soft silt of the rice fields, mingled
With soil from an orange-grove – also

Telephone-wire, and a crane's chain.
Murcia, a surgeon's scalpel and red earth;
Andalucía, the vast south, shall pay
The barrel of a very old rifle found in the hills
Beside a skeleton; earth
That the olives grow from.
And Albacete, where we built our brigades:
Knife-steel and road-dust.

Take then these metals, under the deep sky
Melt them together; take these pieces of earth
And mix them; add your bullets
And memories of death:
You have won victory,
People of Spain
And the tower into which your earth is built, and
    Your blood and ours, shall state Spain's
      Unity, happiness, strength; it shall face the breath
Of the east, of the dawn, of the future, when there will be no more
    strangers ...

August 1937

Thomas O'Brien

The Doomed

It was a time when somebody thought
He would rule the world.
It was a time when establishment
Was under pressure,
When worried parents worried
Because their children danced with strange steps.
Some of them danced their way to Spain
Where it was not dancing time.

I saw one man dancing under fire;
He thought bullets were whizzing under his feet.
He did not die.
The doomed know that bullets strike higher.
They never dance
They become very quiet; you see in their eyes

A lost look, a past look.
There are many who knew they would die
This I swear;
That distant boom meant doom,
That rat-ta-ta had lost its ha-ha-ha.
And the world was small and still,
And the world was sick,
In the stomach and in the brain,
So sick, so sick, you cannot know,
Unless you anticipate the inevitable blow.
Some of them died howling.
Others moaned deep, deep inside them,
You'll say the sound of their moaning
Came from somewhere else,
Not from them, not by them;
And you guessed they were already dead
Gone from this world, from themselves.
Others lay cheerfully on stretchers
Glad of a rest but later you heard
It was eternal.
And we carried on
Haggard, starved, lost in a feverish reality.
In a feverish unreality
You hardly heard the guns;
You got used to it, like traffic
But you knew, you knew
The cursed indifference of bullets
And how you were not at all precious,
Not the least bit valuable,
You could be shattered like a lemonade bottle.

Bob Cooney

Hasta la Vista, Madrid!

Seven and twenty years!
That long?
It seems but yesterday
We left that war torn hill
Above Gandesa

Is it perhaps because I'm growing old
That thought now skips so lightly down the years?
And the travail of a quarter-century
Melts in the vision
Of those great days
Those days we *lived*
And *knew* that we were living

We were at war –
And yet we were at peace
We knew a peace we had not known at home
Where conscience nagged
And conflict raged within us

Spain!
We woke each morning to the thought of Spain
Spain in our thoughts all day
And into each troubled night
Disturbing thoughts
Reproaching thoughts
Home was no longer home
For we were in the rear
While the battle raged at the front

Comrades we'd never seen
Yet knew – and loved –
How dear they had grown –
Leaving their ripening crops
To reap a different, bitter harvest
Fighting a war we knew was rightly ours
Since the fascist poison-weed
Drew sustenance from the rotten soil of Cliveden
Making England a dirty word

England had to be cleansed
So we went to Spain
Where the defeat of Hitler started
– And more than that –
For freedom's an infectious thing
No frontier can contain it

And many a freedom fighter
Who served his stern apprenticeship in Spain
Proved every inch a craftsman
In later battles
In the Hitler rear
In Italy and in France
In the hills of Yugoslavia
In Germany itself

– Even in far off Cuba
Men who had learned their craft in Spain
Communicated skills
To a newer generation
Of freedom fighters
Giving this proof – this guarantee
No freedom fight is ever really lost
While men can learn
Each human mind's an outpost
And the frontiers of freedom expand
Conquering minds and hearts
Prelude to the conquest
Of cities and of states
Till the world is wholly free
Then men will strive for higher freedoms still

What does El Caudillo see today?
As he sits and broods
Lonely and afraid
In his palace – now become a jail
What does he see?

Hitler's gone!
Mussolini's gone!
Batista's gone!
Who goes next ?
Salazar?
– or even …?
Perish the thought
But the thought won't perish

In London today
In Paris today

In Warsaw, Prague, and Rio de Janeiro
There are men and women
Exiled those seven and twenty years

But today
There's a spring in their step
And a meaningful phrase on their lips
A phrase that is *more* than a phrase
It is a promise!
A promise to Spain
To themselves and to each other
And a promise to you Caudillo!

'Hasta la vista, Madrid'
How do you like that promise, Caudillo?
Will you be there?
We'd like to know
For we are coming too

There is so much
We want to see once more
We will stroll in the Puerta del Sol
And the Ramblas of Barcelona
We will cross the Ebro
And drink with our friends in Mora
– Friends who'll be *free*!

We will look at them
And at each other
And each of us will think
This is why I came in '36

And if I live to be a hundred
I'll have this to be glad about
I went to Spain!
Because of that great yesterday
I am part of the greater tomorrow

Hasta la vista, Madrid!

Bill Feeley

Return to Spain

Many years have surged behind us
Since we strode the land of Spain;
And for years beneath the olive trees
Our valiant dead have lain.

But the years go on unending
Young and strong as we were then
For the hungering of freedom
Never dies in the hearts of men.

As the old Brigaders dwindle,
So the young battalions grow,
Striving with our Spanish comrades
To oppose the common foe.

Soon to Spain we shall return
To celebrate with our dear friends.
When they hail the dawn of freedom
And the long night of hatred ends.

James R Jump

Comrades

*Written after meeting a group of former members of the International
Brigades in the Plaza del Pilar, Saragossa*

Do I really know these men
who shuffle with uncertain steps and,
with pink-rimmed eyes behind necessary glasses,
blink bewilderedly in the raw sunlight
of the Pilar Square?
Their bodies are twisted and bent
beneath their youthful, floral shirts
and some of them limp.
Do I know these men?

Then one of them takes my hand and calls me 'Comrade'.
With that single word
the mists of more than forty years roll by
and blurred images zoom into focus
across time and space ...

Young men far from home,
fast losing the innocence of youth
in the iron frenzy of battle;
dead mules
obscenely spilling their entrails over the road;
shallow plough-furrows that offered us
imaginary safety as the black planes swooped;
the hospital crowded with men wearing plaster
and leaning on crutches;
the thinly-rolled cigarette,
palm-covered against snipers,
passing from hand to hand
round a circle of unshaven faces,
from mouth to mouth,
the deep inhaling
and the sighing out of the acrid smoke ...

More than forty years lie
between what was and what is
but across the chasm of time
I know these men,
for they are part of my past
and, therefore, part of me.
I am one of them,
white-haired, bespectacled and limping.
Through thick glasses I know these men.
I see them not as they are,
crumpled and faded with the weight of years,
but as they were,
carefree and noble in the virility of youth.

I am one of them.
They are my comrades,
my brothers.

David Marshall

I Wish I Were Back ...

I wish I were back in the trenches round Madrid
Along with the chicos, among the strangeness of tongues:
Strong in my body, testing it thus and thus,
Half wondering that my flesh can bear these things.

Glad in my loneliness, wrapt in my alien thoughts;
My quaintness cloaking me, like cold air
Stirring on the skin when putting off familiar clothes –
Just as I stepped out of my time-pocked life
Into this.

Then the terror stript me of bewilderment,
Left me shrinking and shell-less, my soul
A slim white worm, curling blindly in fear:
Only one direction to my consciousness,
To kill before I was killed, and glad to die
That our new world begins.

And the tanks lurching like monsters
Stiff-shouldered through the slime,
The horrid black concussion of bombs
Spouting earth skywards,
And the vicious shrapnel
And the hideous chatter of machine-guns
All these could not shatter our resolution.

Thomas O'Brien

'The deserters, all three, complaining'

The deserters, all three, complaining;
One bitter, one pleading, another laying down the law:
Comrades, I said to myself,
I do not care if you desert;
I do not know what it means,
I have not been there.

I respect you as veterans.
I am a boy, a thousand years your junior.

But, of course, I did not know even that,
Even such a simple thing.
One day under fire
I grew a new dimension,
Skin swollen under a shrunken skeleton,
Big outside, small inside, and then I knew
They were actually trying to kill me
With real bullets.
A few days later bullets were normal
And I knew men died and I knew
My licence to live had expired.
I could be that shape
One of those ticked off a list:
Number three company is rapidly declining.
A few days later I was an apprentice veteran –
Sick and silent.

But when I was told to guard these three
I was a boy and yet I sensed
A difference, I sensed they sensed
A difference, for after a while one of them said:
You don't know what it's like.
Sad stinging words, accusing me
Of being innocent, and not in the right place
Guarding them, veterans. I do not know
What happened to them.
I do not know what happened to many others
That passed up and down those arid hills.
But I remember being innocent
And those men I guarded
Who had lost their innocence.

1974

Hugh Sloan

A Tribute

Jumping the skies and time in search of our future
The plane slips evenly forward through the dark night.
Just a short flip and we are there.
Yesterday, when we were young, the trip was longer and devious
And our cause lay footsore over the mountains and through the valleys.
Like a gathering storm we came as droplets, mountain streams then
    raging torrents
And the fury was heard all over the Earth and stirred its sympathy.
Fascism was striding across Europe and the brave Spanish people
    were breaking the shackles of feudalism.
Guernica was calling for revenge and humanity responded and sent
    its sons.
We became one people defending the homes of Spain and our own
Against a murdering pestilence that threatened a thousand years of
    enslavement
Serving in a People's Army for a people's cause.
There was no other way we could go.
With idealism in our minds, we were no idealists,
With passion in our hearts, we were no romantics,
With fire in our bellies, we were no warriors.
We were doing the job that life had thrust upon us.

Ewart Milne

Channel Spray

What do they make of Ireland,
Of Fianna girls and Fianna boys?
De Valera, Lemass and Brooke
What do they make of Ireland?
    Said the man in the militia jacket
    That he got in the war in Spain.

Do they break the stone in Ireland
As when they cheered Parnell?
Are the factories closed against them
For whom Jim Connolly fell?

No sound I hear but silence
Speaking louder than any band,
And Irishmen as channel spray
Labouring in neighbour England.

But neither Gael nor Saxon
Have found their liberty,
Nor will unless they build a bridge
Of unity, by unity.

So proudly then might Ireland
Send her children oversea,
And Fianna girls and Fianna boys
Dance on England's pleasant lea.

And they'll wear the English posies
The Kent and Surrey may,
And English lads wear Irish green
For ever and a day
  Said the man in the militia jacket
  That he got in the war in Spain.

James R Jump

Joe Monks

International Brigader 1914-1988

It is all over now –
the funeral orations,
the singing,
the poems dedicated to your memory
and the slow, Celtic strains of the sad violin.
If you could have heard the praise
bestowed on you, Joe,
you would have blushed inside your coffin
but all the praise was well deserved.

It is all over now –
the sandwiches eaten,

the cups and plates washed and put away,
your friends and relations all back home
in England or in Ireland.
It is all over now
and we have nothing but vivid memories
which will finally fade.

It is all over now.
You are at peace, Joe.
You have left behind life's worries,
its sadness and its joys.
you have also left behind
an example to be followed by others.
There will be no oblivion for you Joe.
Your name will forever be linked
with your comrades in arms –
Ralph Fox, John Cornford,
Frank Conroy, Michael Nolan and Tommy Woods.

It is all over now.
It is over for you, Joe,
but not for me.
Now that it is all over,
I shall start to miss you.

18 January 1988

David Marshall

I Have Lived in a Time of Heroes

I have lived in a time of heroes
And heroines; of great objectors
To subjection and persecution.

I have rubbed rough shoulders
With unnumbered unknown soldiers
Dead in their tens of thousands.

The working men who saved Madrid,
Those lads that fell at Alamein
At Arnhem and at Stalingrad.

These were my comrades, my companions,
Civilians, conscripts, partisans,
Who did great deeds to win hard victory.

In unremembered graves they lie
Untrumpeted, their songs forgotten
Our children are not taught their history.

And you forget them at your peril
For though you fight as well as they
You'll be betrayed, as we were.

Sketch by Clive Branson of fellow International Brigaders in the prisoner of war camp, Palencia, in 1938. *Courtesy Rosa Branson*

About the poets

Valentine Ackland, writer and journalist, was born in London in 1906 and lived in East Chaldon, Dorset. She and Sylvia Townsend Warner were invited to Barcelona by Tom Wintringham in September and October 1936, where they worked in the offices of the newly arrived British Medical Unit. Ackland and Warner also visited Spain in July 1937, attending an international congress of writers sympathetic to the Republic. She died in 1969.

Clive Branson, artist and writer, was born in India in 1907 and studied at the Slade School of Fine Art, London – at the same time as Felicia Browne, the sculptress, who in August 1936 became the first British volunteer to be killed in Spain. He lived in Battersea, south London, where he was active in the Aid Spain movement after Franco's insurrection. He arrived in Spain in January 1938 and joined the British Battalion. He was captured at Calaceite, in Aragón, in March and imprisoned until repatriation in late October of that year. He was killed in action in Burma on 25 February 1944 while serving with the 25th Dragoons, Royal Armoured Corps.

Norman Brookfield, born in 1914 in Kelvedon, Essex, was an assistant librarian in Billericay when he went to Spain in May 1938. He was a company clerk in the British Battalion's No.1 'Major Attlee' Company and transferred to No.4 Company for the Ebro offensive that summer. He was killed in action in the Sierra de Caballs on 23 September 1938, the final day that the battalion was involved in front line fighting.

Frank Brooks, born in 1914, was an accounts clerk from Streatham, south London. He entered the International Brigades in December 1937 and was repatriated with the British Battalion in December of the following year. Nothing more is known about his life.

Ralph Cantor was the name used by Ralph Cantorovitch in Spain. He was born in Manchester in 1916 and worked as a commercial traveller before making his way to Spain in November 1936. With the anglophone No.1 Company of the French La Marseillaise Battalion, he was sent to the fronts at Lopera in December 1936 and Las Rozas in January 1937. He afterwards served with the British Battalion at Brigade HQ at Morata de Tajuña during the battle of Jarama before being assigned to the No.2 Machine Gun Company in June 1937. He died a few weeks later around 8/9 July as a result of stomach wounds sustained at Mosquito Ridge during the Brunete offensive.

Bob Cooney, born in 1907, was a pawnbroker's clerk in Aberdeen, where he became active in the Communist Party. He studied at the Lenin School, Moscow, in 1931/2 and arrived in Spain in September 1937. He was the British Battalion's political commissar from April 1938 and was repatriated with most of the remainder of the battalion in December 1938. He was blacklisted by building trade employers in

Bob Cooney (foreground), pictured with other British Battalion volunteers, including Sam Wild (front row, right). *Courtesy Marx Memorial Library*

Aberdeen after the Second World War and lived in Birmingham for about fifteen years. He died in 1984.

John Cornford was born in 1915 in Cambridge, where he later read history. He left for Spain in August 1936, first fighting with the militia of the POUM (Partido Obrero de Unificación Marxista) at the Aragón front. He returned to England to find recruits for the newly formed International Brigades, arriving back in Spain with a group of over twenty volunteers in October. With the anglophone section of the XI Brigade, he took part in actions in the defence of Madrid at Casa de Campo and University City, where he received a shrapnel wound to the head. Transferred to the No.1 Company of the La Marsellaise Battalion, on Christmas Day he was sent to the front at Lopera, near Córdoba, where he was killed on 28 December 1936.

Charles Donnelly was a Dublin-based journalist, poet and Irish Republican, born in Dungannon, Co Tyrone, in 1914. He was twice gaoled for his trade union activities, in 1934 and 1935, after which he moved to London, where he joined the Spanish Medical Aid Committee following the outbreak of the civil war. He arrived in Spain in January 1937 and soon after enlisting with the British Battalion transferred to the Abraham Lincoln Battalion along with most of the other volunteers from Ireland. He was killed on 27 February 1937 in the abortive attack on Pingarrón Hill during the battle of Jarama.

Courtesy Joseph Donnelly

John Dunlop, a chartered accountant, was born in 1915 in Winnipeg, Canada, but was living in Edinburgh when he volunteered to join the International Brigades in May 1937. He suffered a shrapnel wound at Brunete in July of that year and, on recovery, was sent to the International Brigades' training base at Tarazona de la Mancha. He rejoined the No.2 Machine Gun Company of the British Battalion and saw action at Fuentes de Ebro in October 1937, Teruel early in 1938, the crossing of the Ebro in July 1938 and the ensuing battle until September, when the battalion was withdrawn. He returned to Britain in December with the rest of the battalion. A recollection of his experiences appeared in *Voices from the Spanish Civil War: Personal Recollections of Scottish Volunteers in Republican Spain 1936–39*.[1] Until his retirement he ran a printing business in Edinburgh. He died in 2006.

Eric Edney was twenty-nine when he arrived in Spain in January 1937. Originally from Wootton Rivers, Wiltshire, he was working as a clerk and living in Peckham, south London, when he joined the International Brigades. He was wounded at Jarama and later worked at the British Battalion's post office. After the war he worked as a journalist and co-edited the International Brigade Association's journal, *Spain Today*, along with Lon Elliott. He died in 1989.

Lon Elliott was born in Ipswich in 1912 and read modern languages at Cambridge University. He had worked as a teacher and as the manager of a bookshop by the time he left for Spain in March 1937. Arrested at St Gaudens along with other volunteers making their way to Spain, he spent six weeks in a French jail. He eventually crossed the Pyrenees in May and enlisted with the British Battalion. He worked first as an interpreter for company political commissar George Brown during the fighting at Brunete. After Brown's death in July 1937, he was posted to Madrid where he worked on the staff of the XV Brigade newspaper *Volunteer for Liberty*. He left Spain in February 1939 but remained in Paris for some time to organise the repatriation of volunteers. Afterwards, with Eric Edney, he edited the International Brigade Association's journal, *Spain Today*, and worked as a journalist. He died in 1982.

Bill Feeley, born in 1914, worked as a laboratory assistant at a glass factory in St Helens, Lancashire. He arrived in Spain in August 1937 and saw action at Fuentes de Ebro in October of that year and at the battle of the Ebro, in which he was wounded in the thigh in September 1938. He returned to Britain in December 1938 and in the postwar years worked in the construction industry. Until his death in 1977 he was active on Merseyside in the Constructional Engineering Union, later to become the Constructional Division of the Amalgamated Engineering Workers' Union.

George Green was a professional cellist, born in Stockport in 1904. He drove an ambulance to Spain in February 1937 and was after

George Green plays the cello, with Nan Green on accordion, at the hospital at Huete. *Courtesy Marx Memorial Library*

wards employed as a dispatch rider, hospital orderly and administrator. He served at the front at Casa de Campo, Jarama, Segovia and Brunete and in December 1937 joined the British Battalion's infantry. He was wounded in August 1938 in the Sierra de Pandols during the battle of the Ebro but quickly returned to the front line, only to be killed in the Sierra de Caballs on 23 September during the battalion's last day in action. His widow, Nan Green (1904-84), from Beeston, Nottinghamshire, was working as a hospital administrator in Spain at the time, having arrived in September 1937, and after the war became the secretary of the International Brigade Association. Her autobiography, *A Chronicle of Small Beer: The Memoirs of Nan Green*, was published posthumously in 2005.[2]

Bill Harrington, born in London in 1915, described himself as a 'jack-of-all-trades' when he arrived in Spain in January 1937, having been an RAF pilot, journalist and seaman. He was with the British Battalion at the battle of Jarama and was wounded at Belchite in September 1937. Promoted to sergeant in the No.2 Machine Gun Company in April 1938, he was wounded at Hill 481 near Gandesa during the Ebro offensive in July and remained in hospital until mid-

October, returning to Britain in December 1938. Nothing more is known about the remainder of his life.

Jim Haughey, born in 1919, hailed from Lurgan, Co Armagh. He joined the British Battalion soon after arriving in Spain in May 1938. In September he was captured in the Sierra de Caballs during the battle of the Ebro and was not released from the prison camp at San Pedro de Cardeña until April 1939. He travelled to Vancouver, Canada, immediately afterwards and in 1941 volunteered for the Royal Canadian Air Force. He died on a training mission on 12 September 1943.

Tony Hyndman, from Cardiff, was a former Guardsman and aged twenty-five when he joined the British Battalion in December 1936, having been employed as poet Stephen Spender's secretary while living in Hammersmith, west London. At the battle of Jarama he was a runner for the No.2 Machine Gun Company. He was arrested in Valencia in March 1937 after deciding to go home rather than return to the front and was imprisoned at Albacete. He was released and repatriated in August after Spender interceded with the Communist Party leadership in Britain. He became a pacifist and conscientious objector during the Second World War. He worked in the theatre as a stage manager and director and later as a social worker in Cardiff – where he was known as Tommy Hyndman. He wrote about his time in Spain in *The Distant Drum: Reflections on the Spanish Civil War*.[3] He died in 1982.

James R Jump was born in Wallasey, then part of Cheshire, and was a twenty-one-year-old reporter on the *Worthing Herald* when he travelled to Spain in November 1937. He was assigned to paymaster and interpreter duties at the British Battalion base at Tarazona de la Mancha. In May 1938 he transferred to the No.2 Machine Gun Company and in August received a shrapnel wound in the hand at Hill 666 in the Sierra de Pandols during the Ebro offensive. Following hospital treatment he returned to Britain in December 1938. He later married a Spanish Republican refugee and taught and wrote books about the Spanish language, including *La ofensiva del Ebro*,[4] and *The Penguin Spanish Dictionary*, which was published in 1990, shortly before his death. He was the secretary of the International Brigade Memorial Appeal, which raised the funds to erect the International Brigade memorial unveiled in Jubilee Gardens in London's South Bank in 1985. He wrote about his experiences in the civil war in *The Distant Drum: Reflections on the Spanish Civil War.*[5]

Courtesy Kathy Lee

Laurie Lee was born in Stroud, Gloucestershire, in 1914 and had been living in Almuñecar, near Motril, at the time of Franco's military uprising in July 1936. He was evacuated by a British destroyer a few weeks later. He made his own way back to Spain in December 1937 and was initially imprisoned in Figueras before his identity and motives for crossing the Pyrenees were confirmed. He was taken to the British Battalion base at Tarazona de la Mancha and, because of his epilepsy, given clerical work. He was discharged on medical grounds in January 1938, but in Barcelona again found himself under arrest for a few days until *Daily Worker* correspondent Bill Rust helped secure his release. He left Spain in the following month. Lee subsequently achieved fame as a writer, with the first of a series of autobiographical novels published in 1959. A memoir based on his time in Spain during the civil war, *A Moment of War*, was published in 1991, six years prior to his death.[6]

John Lepper was a twenty-four-year-old journalist already in Spain when he volunteered to join the International Brigades in late 1936. He gave as his address a pub in London's Fleet Street. For medical reasons he was at first assigned to non-combat duties and worked as a chauffeur, but he was later ordered to the front during the fighting at Jarama in February 1937. Traumatised by the battle, he was arrested in Valencia, along with Tony Hyndman, in March, having left his unit without permission and was imprisoned at Albacete. He was repatriated in September later that year. Further information about his life is unavailable.

Alex McDade, a labourer from Glasgow, arrived in Spain in January 1937, aged thirty-two, and was wounded while serving with the British Battalion at the battle of Jarama in the following month. He was a company political commissar when he was killed at Villanueva de la Cañada on 6 July 1937 during the fighting around Brunete.

Tony McLean, born in 1911 in Langwith, Nottinghamshire, was a teacher and writer living in North Kensington, London, when he decided to volunteer for the International Brigades. He arrived in Spain in May 1937 and was found to be unfit for front line service. He undertook clerical work, including censoring mail, and some teaching at the headquarters of the International Brigades in Albacete and with the British Battalion. He returned to Britain in December 1938. In 1945 he was appointed as full-time adult tutor for the University of Oxford, spending

Courtesy Margaret McLean

much of his time teaching in Africa. He later became a senior tutor at the University of Kent at Canterbury. He died in 1982.

David Marshall, born in 1916 in Middlesbrough, worked as a dole office clerk before going to Spain early in September 1936. He joined the anti-fascist militia in Barcelona, where he teamed up with some other early arrivals from Britain. They called themselves the Tom Mann Centuria – after the dockers' union leader – and, with the news that the International Brigades were being created, made their way to Albacete at the end of October. There, they were attached to the mainly German Thaelmann Battalion and immediately deployed to the front near Madrid. In November Marshall received a bullet in the leg while in action at Cerro de los Ángeles and was repatriated in January 1937 after hospital treatment at Albacete. During the Second World War he participated in the Normandy landings in June 1944 and the liberation of Belsen concentration camp in April 1945. In 1961 he moved to London, working as a joiner for theatres and later buying and refurbishing a Thames barge, the *Jock*, which, as well as providing him with an income, hosted several reunions of International Brigade veterans. He died in 2005.

David Martin was born in Budapest, Hungary, in 1915 as Ludwig Detsinyi. He was educated in Germany, which he left in 1934, moving first to the Netherlands and then Palestine. In December 1936 he travelled to Spain and enlisted with the medical service of the XV Brigade, serving at the battles of Jarama, Brunete and Teruel. In 1938 he settled in London to work in his father's clothing factory and later became a journalist with the *Daily Express*, *Reynolds News* and the BBC in Glasgow and London. In 1949 he emigrated to Australia where he pursued a career as journalist and writer. His autobiography, *My Strange Friend*, was published in 1991.[7] He died in 1997.

Ewart Milne was born in 1903 in Dublin and was a merchant navy officer between 1920 and 1935. He worked in the London office of the Spanish Medical Aid Committee and later as a courier for SMAC, travelling between Britain, France and Spain. An autobiographical account of one of his trips to Spain, 'Gun Runner', appeared in his anthology of stories about the Spanish Civil War, *Drums without End*, which was published in 1985, two years before his death.[8]

Joe Monks, born in 1904 in Dublin, settled in Acton, west London, as a young man and worked as a machine operator. He volunteered for the International Brigades in December 1936 and was sent with No.1 Company of the La Marseillaise Battalion of the XIV Brigade from Albacete to Andujar, near the front at Córdoba. He was wounded during fighting at Lopera and remained in hospital at Orihuela until February 1937. He was then transferred to a multinational battalion of the 86th Mixed Brigade and saw action at Chimorra, also on the Córdoba front, and afterwards with the XIV Brigade was sent to the front at Segovia. He returned home in July 1937. He was a committee member of the International Brigade Memorial Appeal, which erected the International Brigade memorial in London's South Bank

Joe Monks (right) on leave in Murcia in 1937. *Courtesy Marx Memorial Library*

in 1985, the same year that his autobiographical account, *With the Reds in Andalusia*, was published.[9] He died in 1988.

Bert Neville, originally from Ipswich, was a fifty-three-year-old taxi-driver from Hammersmith, west London, when he joined the International Brigades in February 1937. He was posted to the Jarama front with the British Battalion and then sent into action at Chimorra on the Córdoba front in April 1937 as part of the Anglo-American No.2 Company of the 86th Mixed Brigade. Wounded at Brunete in July 1937, he spent the next five months in hospital before being medically discharged and returning home. It is not known when he died.

Thomas O'Brien was a Dublin journalist, born in 1914, who arrived in Spain in April 1938. He joined the British Battalion and crossed the Ebro in the Republic's offensive of July and August of that year. He was assigned rearguard duties at the end of August after being wounded and returned home in December 1938. Under the pseudonym of Harry Mancher he later wrote pulp fiction, while continuing to write poems, plays and essays. He also launched his own publishing house. He died in 1974.

Irish International Brigaders, including Thomas O'Brien (foreground, left) are welcomed home at Dun Laoghaire in December 1938. Also pictured (third from right) is Michael O'Riordan. *Courtesy Michael O'Brien*

Pat O'Reilly, born in Thurles, Co Tipperary, in 1908, went to London to work as a bookbinder and also spent some time in the British army. Known as Pat, though his real name was John, he arrived in Spain in early December 1936 and was sent with a group of Irish and British volunteers in the XIV Brigade to the front near Córdoba and fought at Lopera and Las Rozas. He afterwards joined the British Battalion but transferred with most of the other Irish to the Abraham Lincoln Battalion. Subsequently wounded, he was cared for at the hospital at Villa Paz outside Madrid. There he met American nurse Salaria Kea (1917-1990), married her in October 1937 and they honeymooned on the Mediterranean coast before he was repatriated. After the war he settled in the US with Kea, who was the only African-American nurse in Spain. They lived in New York and moved to Akron in 1975, but subsequent details of O'Reilly's life are not known.

Aileen Palmer, born in Australia in 1915, was in Barcelona in July 1936 when the military revolt against the Republic was launched. She had been working as a translator for the People's Olympiad, which the city was to host as a rival to the Berlin Olympics. She was evacuated on a British ship to Marseilles but returned in August to join the newly

Aileen Palmer (centre, in dark top) in unknown location in Spain with other medical staff. *Courtesy Marx Memorial Library*

formed British Medical Unit as an administrator. She served at the front during the defence of Madrid in the winter of 1936/7 and, following a break in London, worked throughout the following winter as the secretary to Len Crome (1909-2001), the Chief Medical Officer of the International Brigades and future chairman of the International Brigade Association. She returned to London in the spring of 1938, where she continued to campaign for the Republic. On 21 January 1939 she threw red ink, representing Spanish blood, over the entrance to 10 Downing Street and was fined 10 shillings and bound over for six months. She served with the London Ambulance Service during the ensuing world war and returned to Australia in 1945, where she remained active as a poet, journalist and linguist, translating Ho Chi Minh's *Prison Diary* into English. She died in 1988.

Hugh Sloan was a Fife miner, born in 1912, who left for Spain in April 1937. Arrested in France and deported to the UK, he entered Spain in May on his second attempt and joined the British Battalion's Anti-Tank Battery, acting as runner, secretary and paymaster. He took part in actions at Jarama, Brunete, Quinto and the crossing of the Ebro. He was repatriated in December 1938. After the war he returned to the pits until 1964 when he was advised to leave through ill-health. He was a gifted artist and contributed satirical sketches to the *Daily Worker* and colliery union papers. He recalled his time in Spain in *Voices from the Spanish Civil War: Personal Recollections of Scottish Volunteers in Republican Spain 1936-39*.[10] He died in 1994.

Miles Tomalin, born in Sanderstead, Surrey, in 1903, was a Cambridge University graduate and worked as an advertising typographer, musician, teacher and journalist. He went to Spain in May 1937 and joined the British Battalion's Anti-Tank Battery. He saw action at Brunete and then in Aragón at Quinto, Belchite, Fuentes de Ebro and Segura de los Baños. He worked on the staff of *Volunteer for Liberty* during the winter of 1937/8. He was back with the British Battalion when it crossed the Ebro in July 1938 and was evacuated to hospital with a blood-poisoned leg a month later. Repatriation came in December 1938 following hospital treatment and convalescence. He resumed his career as a writer and died in 1983.

Sylvia Townsend Warner, novelist and poet, was born in Harrow, Middlesex, in 1893. She worked briefly in the Barcelona offices of the British Medical Unit in the autumn of 1936 along with Valentine Ackland, with whom she lived in East Chaldon, Dorset. The two returned to Spain in July 1937, visiting Madrid as delegates to the congress of the International Association of Writers for the Defence of Culture. She died in 1978.

Tom Wintringham, born in Grimsby in 1898, served as a mechanic and dispatch rider in the First World War. He read history at Oxford and was a founder member of the Communist Party as well as a founder editor of *Left Review*. In 1925, with other party leaders, he was sentenced to one year's imprisonment under the Incitement to Mutiny Act after urging members of the armed forces not to 'turn your guns on your fellow workers'. He later became military correspondent for the *Daily Worker*. He travelled to Barcelona in August 1936 and helped form the Tom Mann Centuria, comprising the few Britons in the city, who later made their way to the International Brigades base at Albacete. In early February 1937 he took over command of the British Battalion and led it at the battle of Jarama until being wounded. He returned to active duties in June, first as an instructor at the newly formed International Brigade officers' training school at Pozorrubio, and then to the front line in Aragón with the British Battalion. He was badly wounded in the shoulder at Quinto in August 1937 and returned to London in November 1938. In the following year, *English Captain*, his account of his experiences in Spain, was published.[11] During the Second World War he was the instigator behind the creation of the Home Guard in 1940. He died in 1949.

Notes

1. *Voices from the Spanish Civil War: Personal Recollections of Scottish Volunteers in Republican Spain 1936-39*, edited by Ian MacDougall, Polygon, Edinburgh 1986.
2. *Chronicle of Small Beer: The Memoirs of Nan Green*, Trent Editions, Nottingham 2005.
3. Op. cit.
4. *La ofensiva del Ebro*, by JR Jump, Harrap, London 1975.
5. Op. cit.
6. *A Moment of War*, by Laurie Lee, Viking, London 1991.
7. Op. cit.
8. *Drums without End: Short stories mainly abut the Spanish Civil War*, by Ewart Milne, Aquila, Portree 1985.
9. *With the Reds in Andalucia*, by Joe Monks, John Cornford Poetry Group, London 1985.
10. Op. cit.
11. *English Captain*, by Tom Wintringham, Faber & Faber, London 1939.

Sketch by Clive Branson of fellow International Brigaders in the prisoner of war camp, Palencia, in 1938. *Courtesy Rosa Branson*

British and Irish volunteers in the Spanish Civil War: a brief history

Spain, July 1936: From uprising to civil war

In July 1936 a military rising was launched in Spain by a group of military generals aiming to overthrow the Republican government, elected only five months previously. Opponents of the rising took to the streets and confronted the insurgents.

With their best soldiers, the elite Army of Africa commanded by General Francisco Franco, trapped in Morocco, the Rebels turned to fascist Italy and Nazi Germany for assistance. Hitler and Mussolini sent help to the Rebels, crucially providing aircraft to ferry the Army of Africa to the peninsula. The Foreign Legionnaires and Moorish troops rapidly headed north, leaving a trail of slaughter and destruction in their wake. Within weeks Franco's forces were approaching Madrid.

Desperate pleas by the Spanish Republican government for assistance from Britain and France fell on deaf ears. Instead, an agreement was made not to intervene in the conflict, to which Britain, France, Germany, Italy, Portugal and the Soviet Union all agreed to adhere. However, it quickly became apparent that the agreement strongly favoured the Rebels, who continued to receive assistance from Germany and Italy.

Appalled at the prospect of another European country succumbing to fascism, supporters of the Spanish Republic from around the world flocked to its aid. At the same time, the Soviet Union chose to provide help to the Republic and the Comintern (Communist International) took on the role of organising the volunteers, many of whom had already arrived in Spain.

Volunteers from Britain, Ireland and the Commonwealth

Between 1936 and 1939 over 35,000 men and women from over fifty countries left their homes to volunteer for the Republican forces. Some 2,300 of these came from Britain, Ireland and the Commonwealth, of whom over 500 were killed.

British and Irish volunteers in Spain: battlefields 1936-1938

1. Lopera, December 1936
2. Boadilla, December 1936
3. Jarama, February 1937
4. Brunete, July 1937
5. Belchite, August-September 1937

6. Teruel, January-February 1938
7. Segura de los Baños, February 1938
8. Calaceite, March 1938
9. Ebro river, July-September 1938

Map: Jeremy Scott

The volunteers came from overwhelmingly working class backgrounds, with large numbers hailing from cities such as London, Manchester, Liverpool and Glasgow. Only a small number were unemployed, with a large proportion involved in industrial occupations, such as labouring, construction, shipbuilding and mining. Their average age was twenty-nine.

With the Thaelmann and Commune de Paris Battalions

In September 1936 a number of British volunteers in Barcelona joined together in an English-speaking unit, the Tom Mann Centuria. By the end of October, after a period of six or seven weeks in which the Centuria took part in no fighting, they welcomed the decision to group foreign volunteers together, which led to their transfer to the town of

Albacete, chosen as the base of the International Brigades, and their official attachment to the mainly German Thaelmann Battalion.

During November, the British group in the Thaelmann Battalion of the XII Brigade was involved in a number of small skirmishes to the south of Madrid, as the Rebels continued their advance on the Spanish capital.

Two weeks before Christmas, the remainder of the battalion was transferred to the village of Boadilla del Monte, to the west of Madrid. But by the time they had arrived, the Republicans were already retreating under a fierce Rebel offensive. In the confusion the English-speaking group became separated from their Spanish comrades and came under intense machine gun fire from a ridge which had earlier been occupied by Spanish Republican soldiers. Seven of the British volunteers were killed.

Meanwhile, British members of the French Commune de Paris Battalion, fighting nearby as part of the XI Brigade, were also suffering heavy losses. During early November they were involved in the defence of the Spanish capital in the Casa de Campo, the park to Madrid's west, and at University City nearby. Many were injured or killed.

By the end of November, the Rebels realised that the Republican forces were now well established, organised and determined and that the direct frontal attack on Madrid had failed.

No.1 Company, La Marseillaise Battalion

By the end of 1936, volunteers were arriving from the British Isles in such numbers that the creation of their own battalion, rather than being attached in small groups to a German or French unit, was becoming a realistic possibility. The first step came in December with the creation of an English-speaking company, as part of the XIV Brigade. The 145-strong British contingent comprised the No.1 Company of the French La Marseillaise Battalion.

On Christmas Eve, the English-speaking company was involved in an attempt to capture the town of Lopera, about thirty miles to the west of Córdoba in southern Spain. Though a number of the company had seen action before, many were completely inexperienced and the company was beaten back by the better armed and trained Rebel forces.

In January 1937, No.1 Company was transferred back to Madrid in an attempt to recapture the Madrid-La Coruña road at Las Rozas. For the poorly equipped and trained volunteers, it was to be a similarly fruitless exercise. As injuries mounted, the English-speaking volunteers were withdrawn and sent to Madrigueras, near Albacete, to join up with recent arrivals from Britain and Ireland.

Formation of the British Battalion

By January 1937 the English-speaking contingent at Madrigueras numbered around 450, enough to form a battalion. However, plans received a setback when many of the Irish volunteers, who had a strongly Irish Republican background and were unhappy about taking orders from ex-members of the British army who had served in Ireland, elected instead to fight with the American volunteers.

Nevertheless, the remainder were formed into the British Battalion and on 9 February the 500-odd members of the battalion left Madrigueras and were transferred to Chinchón, about fifteen miles from Madrid to the south. Here they would confront Franco's crack Moorish troops in a desperate battle at the Jarama Valley, to prevent the Rebels from cutting the vital road between Madrid and Valencia.

Battle of Jarama

Very early in the morning of 12 February 1937, the British Battalion and other members of the mainly English-speaking XV Brigade were moved up to the heights overlooking the Jarama river at Arganda. Facing troops from the Army of Africa, the battalion's lack of training and equipment took its toll, with the number of casualties growing at an alarming rate. By early afternoon, the battalion was in a desperate position, its flank unprotected, the No.2 Machine Gun Company without ammunition, and numbers decreasing by the minute. The remaining volunteers were faced with little choice but to pull back to the battalion headquarters on the plateau behind them. Rebel forces rushed to occupy their positions, but were quickly forced to duck for cover by the Machine Gun Company which at last managed to load its guns with the correct ammunition. As the first day of the battle came to an end, the battalion found itself with less than half the number that had set out from Madrigueras. Day two was to be no less terrifying.

During the following morning, the battalion fought desperately to hold back the Rebel forces. As their flank once again came under attack, the commander of No.4 Company pulled his soldiers back and the Machine Gun Company situated on a knoll to the battalion's right became isolated and surrounded. Over thirty volunteers were captured and several more lost their lives in an ill-judged attempt to rescue them. Somehow, the remaining volunteers in the battalion held on until nightfall.

On day three, under a sustained attack from a hugely superior force supported by artillery and tanks, the line finally broke. In small disorganised groups, the exhausted volunteers drifted back to the cookhouse, where they were told that they were now the only troops between the Rebels and the Valencia road. Despite their physical and mental exhaustion, 140 volunteers marched back to try to recapture their lost positions. The Rebel soldiers, fooled into believing them to be fresh reinforcements, retreated back to their earlier positions and, during the night of 14/15 February, Republican units were brought up and the gap in the line was finally plugged. Both sides dug defensive fortifications and a stalemate ensued for the rest of the war.

Battle of Brunete

July 1937 saw the British Battalion thrown once more into battle as part of a major Republican offensive designed to relieve pressure on the northern front and break through the Rebels at their weakest point to the west of Madrid. On 6 July, the British Battalion moved towards their objective, the heavily defended village of Villanueva de la Cañada, which Spanish Republican forces had been unable to secure. The battalion was pinned down by well-directed machine gun fire and, forced to take cover, short of water and in temperatures of 40 degrees, waited until nightfall. The village was captured eventually at midnight, though not before a number of volunteers were killed when Rebel soldiers attempted to escape by using civilians as human shields.

The following morning, almost a day behind schedule, the battalion moved forward towards their major objective, the heights overlooking the Guadarrama river, and the village of Boadilla del Monte. But weakened by fatigue, thirst and constant bombardment from the air, they could not advance sufficiently rapidly to capture the unoccupied heights and Rebel forces quickly took the opportunity to move into the position. Of the 331 volunteers in the ranks of the British Battalion at the start of Brunete, only forty-two still remained alive and without injuries.

Into Aragón

In mid-August 1937 the British Battalion was transferred to the Aragón front as part of a Republican campaign aimed at capturing Saragossa and diverting Franco's attention from the northern front where, following the bombing of Guernica and the capture of Bilbao, Santander was coming under threat from the Rebel forces.

The battalion helped capture the town of Quinto at the end of August, but in the process suffered significant casualties. Though the British continued to advance, fighting at Belchite and Mediana, Saragossa remained in Rebel hands and the Republican offensive ground to a halt.

During October, the battalion participated in an over-ambitious plan to capture the town of Fuentes de Ebro, within sight of Saragossa. Attempts to carry infantry on tanks were a lamentable failure. With numbers badly depleted, the battalion was withdrawn for two months for some urgently needed rest.

Teruel and Segura de los Baños

In mid-December 1937, the Republicans launched another Aragón offensive, which captured Teruel. However, by mid-January 1938, their forces were fighting desperately to contain a major Rebel counter-attack and the International Brigades were rushed up to the front.

On 17 January 1938, the British Battalion moved into position, struggling through bitter cold and several feet of snow. Despite a ferocious Rebel artillery bombardment, the battalion held its ground and brought the counter-attack to a halt.

The battalion was commended for its dogged defence of Teruel, but the cost was very high: twenty-one British volunteers were killed in this action, thirteen of them from the No.1 'Major Attlee' Company which had borne the brunt of the Rebel artillery barrage. The depleted British force was withdrawn, but their period of rest and recuperation was to be short-lived, as the Rebel counter-attack gained momentum.

On 16 February, the battalion advanced on Segura de los Baños, forty miles north of Teruel, in a diversionary attack aimed at drawing Rebel attention away. Despite some initial success, the Rebels' superior numbers soon told and the battalion was forced back. Teruel was recaptured by the Rebels shortly afterwards.

The retreat through Aragón

Early in March 1938, Franco launched a massive and well-prepared attack on the Republican forces in Aragón. What began as a series of breakthroughs for the Rebels swiftly became outright retreat for the weary Republican forces as their lines virtually collapsed. The British Battalion was forced to make a fighting retreat through, in turn, Belchite, Lecera, Vinaceite and Caspe. By 15 March, Caspe too was surrendered, despite desperate fighting. Only when the battalion reached Batea and Republican reinforcements were brought up was the Rebel advance checked.

The respite was brief, for on 30 March the Rebels launched another offensive, this time in the south of Aragón. The battalion was marching from Corbera towards Calaceite when disaster struck. Mistaking Italian tanks for Republican units, the battalion was attacked and a large number of the No.1 'Major Attlee' Company were forced to surrender, with many others killed and injured. What was left of the battalion, only eighty volunteers, made their way back to Gandesa. Here they attempted to delay the Rebels as best they could, before retreating back over the river Ebro at Cherta at the beginning of April. With the bridges across the river blown, the Rebel advance was at last stemmed.

The Ebro offensive

To the surprise of many, Republican forces would soon return across the Ebro, in perhaps the most audacious offensive of the entire war. Following a period of desperate reorganisation and training, the battalion was informed on 21 July 1938 that Republican forces were to cross the river in a huge offensive and that the battalion was charged with capturing Gandesa, through which they had retreated months earlier.

After crossing the river during the night of 25 July the battalion made rapid progress, capturing the town of Corbera late that evening, and preparing to move on Gandesa the following day. However, as the Rebels brought up reinforcements and intensified their bombing of the Republican forces, the offensive began to get bogged down. Attempts by the battalion to capture the heavily fortified Hill 481, strategically overlooking Gandesa, proved costly. By 3 August the Republicans gave up their attempt to capture the town, and the battalion was moved into reserve.

James R Jump (back row, second from right) with other volunteers from
the British Battalion in Marsa, July 1938, before the Ebro offensive.
Courtesy Jim Jump

On 24 August, the British Battalion took over the exhausted American positions on Hill 666, the main height of the Sierra de Pandols, near Gandesa. Here the volunteers endured a massive artillery bombardment and an attack by two Rebel battalions. Two weeks later, the battalion moved up to Hill 356 near Sandesco, in the nearby range of Sierra de Caballs, which they managed to capture despite overwhelming numbers of Rebel soldiers and unrelenting artillery and aircraft bombardments.

On 21 September 1938, Juan Negrín, the Spanish prime minister, announced the Republic's intention to repatriate all foreign volunteers. But the battalion was called upon one last time and replaced elements of the XIII Brigade which had suffered heavy losses at Sierra de Lavall de la Torre. After sustaining an immense five-hour artillery barrage, the battalion was caught in murderous Rebel crossfire until the trenches were overrun. When the battalion was withdrawn in the evening of 23 September 1938 the losses of the previous three days were realised: over 200 members of the battalion were killed, wounded, or missing. It was a tragic and heartbreaking end to their role in Spain.

The British Anti-Tank Battery

The British Anti-Tank Battery was formed in May 1937 from forty volunteers at Madrigueras and issued with three Soviet 45mm guns, capable of firing both armour-piercing and high explosive shells which, at that time, represented state-of-the-art military technology. Well led, trained by Russian instructors and comprising a high proportion of students and intellectuals, they represented somewhat of an élite unit, and quickly became a highly efficient force of the XV Brigade.

After cutting its teeth at Brunete in July 1937, the battery was heavily involved in the battles at Quinto and at Belchite.

During the Aragón retreats in the spring of 1938 the battery was virtually surrounded and forced to retreat swiftly from Belchite to avoid being cut off. The battery had to destroy one of its guns could not be moved; low flying Rebel aircraft destroyed another. With the battery no longer in existence, the men were incorporated into the British Battalion.

The medical services

Within a month of the outbreak of war in July 1936, supporters of the Spanish Republic in Britain had established the Spanish Medical Aid Committee. The committee collected money for the Republic and established a hospital at Grañen, near Huesca. During early 1937, the British Medical Unit was incorporated into the Republican 35th Division, which also included the XV Brigade and its British Battalion.

Working in extremely basic conditions and under tremendous pressure, the volunteers in the medical unit were able to save countless lives, though a number of the unit sacrificed theirs in the process. Techniques developed in the war, particularly the storage of blood for transfusions and methods of dealing with fractures and associated wounds after surgery, continued to save lives in the Second World War.

View sketched by Clive Branson at the prisoner of war camp in Palencia.
Courtesy Rosa Branson

Prisoners of war

The members of the No.2 Machine Gun Company captured at Jarama in February 1937 expected to be executed. Indeed three were. After interrogation and finger-printing, the surviving prisoners were taken to an old factory in Talavera de la Reina, where they stayed for three months, repairing roads and burying the bodies of executed Republican prisoners, with little food and the most basic living and sanitary facilities. Several prisoners were still carrying the wounds they had sustained at Jarama; many of the others fell ill from stomach and lung diseases.

In May the prisoners were moved to Salamanca, where they were all tried by a military court for 'aiding a military rebellion'. Five were sentenced to death and the remainder given twenty-year sentences. Following the show trial, they were informed that Franco had pardoned them and that they were to be exchanged for a similar number of Italians captured by Republican forces. Of the twenty-three released British prisoners, five were back in Spain fighting with the British Battalion within six weeks. A small number of prisoners were not released immediately, but were finally freed in November.

A number of volunteers were taken prisoner during the Aragón campaigns of 1938, with over 100 volunteers captured at Calaceite at the end of March. The prisoners were taken to Saragossa for interrogation, where one was recognised as one of the prisoners at Jarama and was taken away and executed for contravening an agreement not to return to Spain.

The other prisoners were transferred to the prison camp of San Pedro de Cardeña, eight miles south-east of Burgos. Conditions were brutal, violence by the guards was endemic, living facilities were overcrowded and unsanitary, and food and medical facilities were woefully inadequate.

In late October about 100 prisoners were freed, with further groups released in February and April 1939, in exchange for Italians held by the Republicans. The last remaining British prisoner was released in March 1940.

Farewell to the International Brigades

The depleted ranks of British volunteers did not leave Spain immediately. On 17 October 1938, all the foreign volunteers in the 35th

Division were paraded and reviewed, and several of their number received promotions and commendations.

The final appearance of the battalion was at a farewell parade in Barcelona at the end of October, at which important Republican figures, including president Manuel Azaña and prime minister Juan Negrín, expressed their thanks to the international volunteers. The speech by Dolores Ibárruri, the Communist deputy from the Asturias forever known as La Pasionaria, was the highlight of an emotional occasion.

Most of the British volunteers, 305 in total, left Spain by train at the beginning of December 1938. They arrived back in London's Victoria Station on the evening of 7 December where they were met by a huge crowd, including Clement Attlee, the leader of the Labour Party, and other senior members of the British labour movement.

For many of the veterans of the International Brigades, the struggle against fascism would continue. Many (where they were accepted) fought in the Second World War and many joined the International Brigade Association, which continued to press for a return to democracy in Spain.

The British Battalion in 1938. *Courtesy IBMT*

Notes on the poems

Every effort has been made to seek permission for publication and to acknowledge the source of each poem. Where this has proved impossible, we would welcome further information so that proper acknowledgement can be given in any further edition.

Spanish spellings have been corrected in poem texts, although anglicised place-names have been retained whenever used by the poet.

Where a poem is untitled, the first line or phrase is used as the heading within quotation marks.

Frontispiece

This is an extract from an anonymous poem lodged as loose sheets in the Working Class Movement Library, Salford. The poem, which runs to over 200 lines, is titled 'In Memoriam George Brown' and is a eulogy to the eponymous International Brigader, born in 1906 in Thomastown, Co Kilkenny, who was a full-time Communist Party organiser in Manchester. He went to Spain in January 1937 and, having served in the British army, was soon promoted to major and company political commissar. He was killed on 7 July 1937 at Villanueva de la Cañada during the Brunete offensive, when the Rebels attempted to break out of the village using women and children as shields. Brown's widow, Evelyn, later married fellow International Brigader Jack Jones.

There are no clues to the poem's authorship, but it was apparently written in 1946:

The ravaged fields
Have nine times grown wheat.
'Tis nine years ago
That George Brown was killed.

Parts of the poem were reproduced in *Poesía anglonorteamericana de la guerra civil española*, edited by Ramón López Ortega and Román Álvarez Rodríguez, Junta de Castilla y León, Salamanca 1986, and *Into the Heart of the Fire: The British in the Spanish Civil War*, by James K Hopkins, Stanford University Press, Stanford 1998, but it is not known whether the whole poem has ever been published. This is how it begins:

Now you are asked to go away from yourselves,
Away from the street of your life,
From the houses and the rooms of your lives.
Leave behind the voices of your children,
Leave behind the smoke of your chimneys:

Leave it behind:
You are asked to be in another place at another time
To yield yourselves to this journey,
To another sun and to other shadows;
Going from the safe to the unknown,
From the clanging of your tramways
To a distant silence,
From to-day to yesterday
And to a day which has not yet come.
You, you, looking at me, looking at yourselves, wondering:
Man next to man,
Woman next to woman:
You are changed now, changed,
Come away, come away.
This is to-day: a bad day, a day of dying.
And a good day when life
Is given a push to live more swiftly
More lively!
To-day it is very hot.
The heat is on your lips, on your tongues…
To the north – look closely! Brunete.
Nearer, nearer, a cluster of white houses, open; Villanueva de la Cañada.
There are parched fields, some trees, a road, telegraph poles,
Dust and thirst and a surge.
This is Spain. The white houses
Are Spain's white houses
On the crossroads in Spain.
The fields are Spanish fields
The telegraph lines run
To Ávila and Segovia.
The serge is the old serge
The same surge, the new surge,
To grow, to break out, to be free,
To be more happy, to live.
Up the road lorries move, carefully.
In extended order, through the dry fields men go, slowly.
What do they carry?
Rifles.
The sun burns their shoulders.
Earlier there was the roaring of guns,
But now they are stilled.
You, you are going forward.
Forward, forward, adelante, adelante!
Your faith is no longer
In your hands, in your heart, on your lips:
It is in your fingers, in your stomach, in your aching feet.
How hot this day is, those white – white houses!
And who is the next man, the man next to you?
Staring ahead at the white houses of Villanueva?
This one, yes, this one…
He turns his face, his eyes – yes.
George Brown.

Clive Branson *December 1936, Spain* page 31
A different version appeared in *The Penguin Book of Spanish Civil War Verse* (op. cit.). This one is transcribed from Branson's journal.

Miles Tomalin *Alès* page 32
Previously unpublished.

Alès is a town near Nîmes on the road south from Paris to the Mediterranean and Spain.

Tony McLean *Sunrise in the Pyrenees, May 1937* page 32
Previously unpublished.

Valentine Ackland *Badajoz to Dorset, August 1936* page 33
From *Women's Voices from the Spanish Civil War*, edited by Jim Fyrth and Sally Alexander, Lawrence & Wishart, London 1991; reproduced by permission of Carcanet Press Ltd.

In August 1936, Badajoz, the chief city of Extremadura, was the scene of savage Francoist repression in which some 2,000 civilians were herded into the bullring and machine-gunned by Falangist irregulars and the Foreign Legionnaires and Moors of the Army of Africa, led by Colonel Juan Yagüe. The crime was exposed by reporters who entered the city from Portugal, including the *Chicago Tribune's* Jay Allen. The bullring massacre was not an isolated incident. Since Franco's death, the names of 6,610 civilians murdered after the military rebellion in just the western half of the province of Badajoz have been identified. See Paul Preston's *The Crimes of Franco* (op. cit.).

Eric Edney *Salud!* page 33
First published in *Volunteer for Liberty*, May 1940. A note adds: 'This poem was written in Spain, and is now published in Britain for the first time.'

'Salud', a familiar form of greeting, was popular among supporters of the Spanish Republic eager to flatten distinctions of hierarchy and rank. See also the poem 'Salud, Brigade – Salud!' on page 83.

Sylvia Townsend Warner *Journey to Barcelona* page 34
From *Sylvia Townsend Warner Selected Poems*, Carcanet Press, Manchester 1985; reproduced by permission of Carcanet Press Ltd.

John Cornford *Full Moon at Tierz: Before the Storming of Huesca* page 35
First published in *Left Review*, March 1937; from *John Cornford: A Memoir*, edited by Pat Sloan, Jonathan Cape, London 1938; reprinted by permission of The Random House Group Ltd.

'Seventh Congress' refers to the Comintern's (Communist International's) Seventh Congress held in Moscow in July 1935 which adopted the policy of anti-fascist 'popular front' alliances with political parties of the centre and left. A popular front coalition had won the Spanish general election in February 1936.

'Oviedo mauser' is a Spanish rifle.

Georgi Dimitrov was the Bulgarian Comintern agent who was charged by the Nazis with plotting a fire at the Reichstag (parliament building) in Berlin in 1933. He successfully defended himself and was acquitted at a trial in Leipzig.

Maurice Thorez was the leader of the French Communist Party and considered to be the architect of the popular front policy.

Oranienburg was the site of one of the Nazis' first concentration camps.

Frank Brooks *'Like molten gold the sun on high'* page 37
First published in *Britons in Spain* (op. cit.).

Thomas O'Brien *Beauty Is Found To Be Ugly* page 38
First published in *Strong Words, Brave Deeds: The Poetry, Life and Times of Thomas O'Brien*, edited by Gustav H Klaus, The O'Brien Press, Dublin 1994.

Clive Branson *The International* page 39
First published in *Poetry and the People*, February 1940.

The 'Internationale' – as it is more usually known – was written by Frenchman Eugene Pottier in 1871 at the time of the Paris Commune and became the anthem of the communist movement around the world. An International Brigade battle songbook published in Madrid 1937 offers eleven different language versions, of which the first verse of the one ascribed to 'USA and England' is:

Arise you prisoners of starvation
Arise you wretched of this earth,
For justice thunders condemnation,
A better world's in birth.
No more tradition's chains shall bind us
Arise you slaves, no more in thrall
The earth shall rise on new foundations
We have been nought, we shall be all.

Chorus:
Then comrades, come rally,
And the last fight let us face,
The International
Unites the human race.

However, the more commonly used British lyrics appeared in another International Brigade songbook, issued a year later in Barcelona. Under the heading 'England', the song begins:

Arise! ye starvlings from your slumbers!
Arise! ye criminals of want!
For reason in revolt now thunders
And at last ends the age of cant.
Now away with all superstitions,
Servile masses, arise! arise!
We'll change forthwith the old conditions
And spurn the dust to win the prize.

International Brigader and poet John Dunlop describes in *Voices from the Spanish Civil War: Personal Recollections of Scottish Volunteers in Republican Spain 1936-39* (op. cit.) how, after their clandestine crossing of the Pyrenees, he and other volunteers began singing the 'Internationale' immediately over the Spanish frontier. 'Here were we, all young men from really all the nations in Europe, and some from outside Europe as well, joining in this one song in their own language which seemed to express a yearning for the unity of mankind. I find it extremely difficult to explain how exhilarating it was. I don't think I've ever felt the same feeling at any other time in my life.'

The inspirational effect of the 'Internationale' played a part in the battle of Jarama in February 1937. It was sung to rally remnants of the routed British Battalion as they launched a desperate but ultimately successful counter-attack. The singing fooled the Rebels into thinking that reinforcements had arrived, so they retreated and the strategically vital Madrid-Valencia road was saved. See a fuller account in Richard Baxell's *British Volunteers in the Spanish Civil War: The British Battalion in the International Brigades, 1936–1939* (op. cit.).

Anonymous *The Internationalist* page 40
First published in *Volunteer for Liberty*, 1 May 1938, with the authorship given as 'I.B.'.
The acronymed slogan 'U.H.P' stands for Unión de Hermanos Proletarios (Brotherhood of the Working Classes).

John Cornford *A Letter from Aragon* page 40
First published in *Left Review*, November 1936; from *John Cornford: A Memoir* (op. cit.); reprinted by permission of The Random House Group Ltd.
'H.E.' stands for high explosive shells.

Tom Wintringham *Spanish Lesson* page 41
First published in *We're Going On! Poems by Tom Wintringham*, edited by Hugh Purcell, Smokestack Books, Middlesbrough 2006.

Joe Monks *Fuente-O-Venjuna* page 42
First published in *With the Reds in Andalusia* (op. cit.), in which Monks says that he wrote the poem in a letter home in the spring of 1937 while serving at the front north of Córdoba, when the village of Fuente Obejuna was the enemy-held target of a Republican counter-offensive.
Fuenteovejuna is also the title of a play written in 1614 by Lope de Vega, the most prolific playwright of Spain's literary 'Golden Age'. Based on true-life events in 1472, it tells the story of how the people of Fuente Obejuna rise up against their evil overlord, El Comendador, who claims feudal privilege and divine authority to justify his cruel behaviour towards them. The play was among those performed by the Republican government-sponsored La Barraca theatre group, founded in 1931 and led by Frederico García Lorca, which toured remote parts of rural Spain performing classical Spanish dramas.

Bill Harrington *Marching Song of the 2nd Company of the British Battalion* page 42
Sung of course to the tune of the hunting song 'D'ye Ken John Peel?', this was first published in *Volunteer for Liberty*, 7 July 1938.
'Queipo' is General Gonzalo Queipo de Llano y Serra, who seized Seville for the Rebels at the start of the war and achieved notoriety through his bombastic radio broadcasts – many listeners suspected him of being drunk – and the savagery of his repression of Republican supporters after the fall of Málaga early in 1937.
Franco installed himself in Burgos soon after the military uprising, but later transferred his headquarters to Salamanca for his unsuccessful assault on Madrid before returning to Burgos for the offensive against the Republican-held northern enclave in the spring of 1937.

Tom Wintringham *International Brigades* page 43
First published in *We're Going On! Poems by Tom Wintringham* (op. cit.).

George Green *Dressing Station* page 44
Previously unpublished.

Tom Wintringham *Granien* page 46
First published in *Left Review*, January 1937. This version is from *Poems for Spain* (op. cit.).

Grañén, on the Aragón front, was the site of a British Medical Unit field hospital in September 1936.

The line 'Too many people are in love with death' is surely a riposte to the notorious outcry of '¡Viva la muerte!' ('Long live death') by one of Franco's closest allies, General José Millán Astray, at the University of Salamanca on 12 October 1936 – three weeks before Wintringham wrote his poem. The interruption came during an address by philosopher Miguel de Unamuno, the university's rector, in which he defended Basque and Catalan nationalism. Unamuno never recovered from the confrontation and ensuing fracas and died less than three months later.

David Marshall *I Have Stood To upon Some Lousy Dawns* page 47
First published in *The Tilting Planet: Poems by David Marshall*, International Brigade Memorial Trust, London 2005.

Eric Edney *The Battalion Goes Forward* page 47
First published in *Volunteer for Liberty*, February 1940.

Edouard Daladier and Neville Chamberlain were the respective prime ministers of France and Britain from April 1938 and May 1937 to 1940 and the architects of the Munich agreement with Hitler and Mussolini in September 1938.

Thomas O'Brien *On Guard for Liberty* page 49
First published in *Workers' Republic*, August 1938. Taken from *Strong Words, Brave Deeds: The Poetry, Life and Times of Thomas O'Brien* (op. cit.).

Pat O'Reilly *A Dying Comrade's Farewell to His Sweetheart* page 49
Previously unpublished.

The poem was sent by John 'Jack' Jolly (1892-1981) in a letter home to his wife in 1937, saying: 'This is from a comrade of mine who I am pleased to say is still with me. He came with me from Paris.' Jolly, a silk-weaver from Burnley, arrived in Spain in December 1936. He was assigned to quartermaster duties, initially in the British Battalion cookhouse and later at the American hospital at Villa Paz outside Madrid and from May 1938 at the hospital in Vich, Catalonia. The poem was in all likelihood acquired when both O'Reilly and Jolly were at the Villa Paz hospital. Was it one of the poems that O'Reilly deployed to woo Salaria Kea?

John Cornford *To Margot Heinemann* page 50
First published in *New Writing*, autumn 1937, where it was entitled 'Poem'; from *John Cornford: A Memoir* (op. cit.); reprinted by permission of The Random House Group Ltd.

Cornford met Margot Heinemann at Cambridge in 1934. She wrote the poem 'Grieve in a New Way for New Losses', published in the same issue of *New Writing*, in response to the news of his death.

John Lepper *Battle of Jarama 1937* page 50
First published in *Poems for Spain* (op. cit.).

Charles Donnelly *The Tolerance of Crows* page 51
First published in *Ireland Today*, February 1937. It was also reproduced in *The Book of the XV Brigade*, Commissariat of the XV Brigade, Madrid 1938, which says: 'This prophetic poem was written by Charles Donnelly before he had decided to leave Ireland and join the International Brigades in Spain. He fell charging the Fascist trenches at Jarama on February 27, 1937. His body, shattered by two explosive bullets, was recovered four days later.' Elements of this description are disputed by Donnelly's family, who say that the

poem was written at the front and that his body was recovered nine days later (letter from brother Joseph Donnelly to the editor, 4 July 2005).

Donnelly's reportedly last words, 'Even the olives are bleeding', form the title of his biography (by Joseph O'Connor, New Island Books, Dublin 1992) and were recalled by Irish folk singer-songwriter Christy Moore in 'Viva La Quince Brigada' ('Long Live the Fifteenth Brigade') which first appeared on his 1984 album *Ride On* (WEA 2292404072).

The third verse of the song is:

Even the olives were bleeding;
As the battle for Madrid it thundered on,
Truth and love against the force of evil,
Brotherhood against the fascist clan.

Ralph Cantor '*'Twas postwar stalemate period' page 52
The poem was, according to Cantor's letters home, which are lodged, along with the poem itself, at the Working Class Museum Library, Salford, written around April 1937. It appears not to have been previously published.

'No pasarán' ('They shall not pass'), a slogan first used during the defence of Madrid early in the war, became the great rallying cry for the Republic's supporters.

Tommy Hyndman *Jarama Front* page 55
First published in *Poems for Spain* (op. cit.).

Lon Elliott *Jarama* page 55
While working at the International Brigades' offices in Madrid, Elliott helped compile *The Book of the XV Brigade* (op. cit.), where this poem was first published.

Alex McDade *Valley of Jarama* page 56
First published in *The Book of the XV Brigade* (op. cit.).

Written after the battle of Jarama and while the British contingent was being kept at the front until June with barely any rest, it is sung to the tune of the traditional American cowboy song 'Red River Valley'. *The Book of the XV Brigade* noted: 'This song became popular with the XV Brigade in May 1937, the fourth month of their stay in the trenches on the Jarama front... and its humorous cynicism made it popular in all Battalions.'

A second, less sardonic, version was featured in the souvenir booklet for the International Brigade British Battalion National Memorial Meeting in Earls Court, London, on 8 January 1939. It came to be known as the 'Song of the British Battalion' and has continued to be sung at International Brigade commemorative events:

There's a valley in Spain called Jarama,
It's a place that we all know so well,
It is there that we gave of our manhood,
And most of our brave comrades fell.

We are proud of the British Battalion,
And the stand for Madrid that they made,
For they fought like true sons of the soil,
As part of the 15th Brigade.

With the rest of the international column,
In the stand for the freedom of Spain
We swore in that Valley of Jarama
That fascism never will reign.

Now we've left that dark valley of sorrow
And its memories we ne'er shall forget,
So before we continue this reunion
Let us stand to our glorious dead.

The following previously unpublished Spanish translation dates from October 1987 and was a collaborative effort by International Brigade veteran James R Jump and Madrid-based poet Rafael Hernández Rico.

Valle del Jarama / Canción del Batallón Británico

En España, Valle del Jarama,
donde nos conocimos ayer,
al que fuimos llenos de ilusiones
a entregar nuestra vida también.

De nuestro batallón orgullosos,
resistiendo por todo Madrid,
pues luchamos los hijos del pueblo
con la Quince Brigada a morir.

En columnas internacionales,
hombro a hombro con el español,
en el Valle del Jarama juramos
no dar paso al fascismo agresor.

Ahora, lejos de aquel duro valle,
su recuerdo jamás morirá
y, antes de partir, recordamos
los hermanos que allí velarán.

There is also a US variant of the song, which evolved after the war into a defiant lament for the defeat of the Republic. It has been recorded by, among others, Woody Guthrie (as 'Jarama' on *Songs Of The Spanish Civil War*, Volume 2, 1962, Folkways Records FH5437) and more recently by Arlo Guthrie and Pete Seeger (*Spain In My Heart*, 2003, Applesead Recordings APR CD1074). Woody Guthrie's version is structured with a chorus which reverses the outcome of the battle:

From this valley they say we are going
But don't hasten to bid us adieu.
Even though we lost the battle at Jarama
We'll set this valley free 'fore we're through.

Charles Donnelly *Heroic Heart* page 57
First published in *Ireland Today*, July 1937.

Ewart Milne *Thinking of Artolas* page 57
First published in *Letter from Ireland*, by Ewart Milne, The Gayfield Press, Dublin 1940.

Milne links the deaths of poet Charles Donnelly and Izzy (Isidore) Kupchick (Kupchik in the poem), a Canadian Jewish ambulance driver killed in June 1937 near Segovia.

Laurie Lee *A Moment of War* page 59
First appeared in *The Sun My Monument*, by Laurie Lee, The Hogarth Press, London 1944; from *Selected Poems*, by Laurie Lee, Penguin Books, Harmondsworth 1985.

Bill Feeley *Who Wants War?* page 61
First published in *Poetry and the People*, September 1938, with the authorship given as 'William Teeley (Spanish People's Army)' and with an explanation that the poem had arrived in a letter, postmarked 26 August 1938, from Barcelona. There is no record of a William Teeley in the British Battalion, but William 'Bill' Feeley is known to have been with the battalion in Catalonia at the time, having been in Spain for just over a year.
The letter, which was reprinted by *Poetry and the People*, says:

It is very difficult to change the ideology of a lot of people in whose minds war and romance are perhaps vaguely but insistently, nevertheless, interrelated. I have had twelve months of modern warfare. I have the good fortune to under-stand exactly what I am fighting for, but that does not make war in the least desirable. That is not to say one wishes to give up the struggle: the agony of a people fighting for liberty is analogous to a Catholic conception of a Purgatory borne willingly for the sake of the Heaven that lies beyond. Well it is my experience which speaks in the enclosed poem and which emboldens me to send it to you, for I consider experience alone can create a proper conception of war.

An editorial commentary said that the letter and poem were 'deeply inspiring' and added: 'That a man who has fought through a year of modern warfare expresses himself naturally in poetry is eloquent of the power poetry has.'

Anonymous *'Munitions men'* page 61
First published in *Volunteer for Liberty*, 13 December 1937. The lines are unatributed, but it may be worth noting that Miles Tomalin was working on the staff of the newspaper at the time.

Bill Harrington *Aragon Ballad* page 61
First published in *Volunteer for Liberty*, 6 October 1938.

John Dunlop *Brunete, 12 July 1937: An Ode to My Comrades* page 62
First published in *IBMT Newsletter*, September 2003.
The poem was memorably read out by Dunlop on 11 October 2003 at the rededi-cation of the La Pasionaria memorial in Glasgow. He wrote it after he first returned to Spain in 1975 and visited the Brunete battlefield, where he found the exact spot where he had been wounded and two of his comrades had been killed in July 1937. According to Dunlop, the penultimate three-line stanza is a quotation from the Roman poet Quintus Horatius Flaccus (Horace) – 'for he, too, as a young man volunteered to fight for a cause he thought was right'. He added: 'The difference is that his poem was in effect a monument to himself and his literary achievements and not to his forgotten comrades who died in the battle which he survived.'; (letter dated 10 December 2004 from John Dunlop to the editor).
Dunlop also translated the poem into Spanish and asked that it be included in this anthology:

Brunete 12 de julio de 1937: Oda a mis camaradas

Al lado del camino un yanqui joven
Yace en una camilla
Su cuerpo retorciéndose en tormento
Acribillado a tiros por una ametralladora

Los sanitarios se esfuerzan tiernamente
Su dolor a restañar
Yo estoy de pie
Mirándolo

Cada célula de mi cuerpo en plena carga
Intentando desesperadamente transmitir corrientes de curación
De mi fuerza a la suya

No puedo quedarme a su lado porque la batalla me llama
A mi propio encuentro en la mañana de la vida

Pronto vainas de acero vuelan por el aire
Preñadas con semillas mortales
Rompiéndose alrededor de mi en el suelo
En instantáneas flores fatales
Floraciones que sacan la vida de mis camaradas, irlandés,
Francés y escocés, yanqui, alemán, español, eslavo, finlandés y ruso
Griego, galés e inglés, árabe, judío y turco
Hombre negro, hombre rojo, rostro pálido
Estuvímos todos allí

Herido, yo me quedo con las piernas de mi camarada tendidas sobre las mías
Su cara, una máscara gris y yerta

El francés se sienta en cuclillas aún, espalda cómoda contra un banco de tierra
Hablando ninguna palabra
Su cabeza se había desvanecido y un poco de sangre ensucia su cuello

Treinta y ocho años más tarde volví a ellos
Donde yacían aún tranquilos y olvidados
Bajo el suelo y el sol
Donde mi sangre mezclábase con la suya
Y con sus huesos alimentaban las hierbas secas y pálidas
Y los arbustillos, a lo largo de los años

Como un guerrero mejicano antiguo
Quebré una de las plantas
Masticando el tallo y tragando el zumo amargo

Entonces los dioses de la guerra y el odio
Rugieron contra nosotros otra vez
Con un estallido de truenos estrepitosos desde las almenas del cielo
Pero todo lo que cayó fueron lágrimas de tésera en gotas dulces
Para humedecerse y mezclarse con las secas mías

Mis camaradas yacían allí en una ladera
Olvidados por todos menos por mi
Sin más memorial que las hierbas secas y pálidas
Y los arbustos pequeños

Pero ahora yo les he erigido un monumento
Más duradero que el bronce
Y más alto que una pirámide

Es éste.

Miles Tomalin *Wings Overhead* page 63
First published in *Volunteer for Liberty*, 27 December 1937.

James R Jump *Sun over the Front* page 64
First published in *With Machine Gun and Pen*, by James R Jump, Alf Killick Educational Trust, Westcliff-on-Sea 1990.

Tom Wintringham *Poem in the Summer of 1937* page 65
First published in the *The Last English Revolutionary: Tom Wintringham 1898-1949*, by Hugh Purcell, Sutton Publishing, Stroud 2004, a biography of Wintringham which tells the story of his love affair with American journalist Kitty Bowler – who inspired this poem – and his consequential expulsion from the Communist Party. The text here is from the version published in *We're Going On! Poems by Tom Wintringham* (op. cit.).

Aileen Palmer *Thaelmann Battalion* page 66
First published in *Poetry and the People*, June 1939; reproduced by permission of State Trustees, Victoria.

The mainly German-speaking Thaelmann Battalion was named after Ernst Thälmann, the leader of the German Communist Party who was arrested by the Nazis in 1933 and held without charge in solitary confinement until being executed at Buchenwald concentration camp in 1944.

Sylvia Townsend Warner *Benicasim* page 67
First published in *Left Review*, March 1938; reproduced by permission of Carcanet Press Ltd.

In Greek mythology the Acheron was the 'river of woe' across which newly dead souls were ferried to the underworld.

See biographical note on Ralph Fox on page 26.

Norman Brookfield *'Rest, I will know your all-pervading calm'* page 68
Probably previously unpublished. The poem is transcribed from a type-written manuscript on file at the Marx Memorial Library, London.

Miles Tomalin *Lull in War* page 68
Previously unpublished.

James R Jump *Ebro Crossing* page 69
Taken from Jump's unpublished bilingual anthology *Poems of War and Peace – Poemas de guerra y paz*, for which Antonio Buero Vallejo (1916-2000), considered by many to be Spain's finest dramatist of the Francoist and post-Franco eras, wrote an introduction under the title 'El poeta cogió su fusil' ('The poet picked up his rifle'). In it, he recalls:

Conviví con muchos brigadistas en nuestra guerra; los he visto cantar, con lágrimas en los ojos, al pisar de nuevo el suelo en que lucharon. Sólo quien haya vivido aquella gesta sabe hasta qué punto es imborrable su recuerdo. El recuerdo que late en la mayoría de los poemas de éste y de otros libros de Jump.

I spent time with many Brigaders during that war. I have seen them singing, tears in their eyes, as they set foot once again on the ground on which they fought. Only someone who lived through those epic times knows how indelibly they are imprinted on the memory. This is the memory which pulsates through most of the poems in this book and in others by Jump.

'Cayetana' was Cayetana Lozano-Díaz, a volunteer helper on the passenger liner *La Habana*, which had arrived in Southampton in May 1937 with nearly 4,000 children from the Basque region seeking sanctuary in Britain during Franco's offensive against the Republic's northern enclave. Jump met her in Lancing, Sussex, where one of the homes for the children had been opened. They were married in 1941.

Miles Tomalin *Down the Road* page 70
First published in *Volunteer for Liberty*, January 1940.

Tony McLean *Full Moon over Barcelona, 1938* page 71
Previously unpublished.

Bill Harrrington *To a Fallen Comrade* page 71
First published in *Volunteer for Liberty*, 5 September 1938.

Thomas O'Brien *International Brigade Dead* page 72
First published in *New Irish Poets: Representative Selections from the Work of 37 Contemporaries*, edited by Devin A Garrity, Devin-Adair Company, New York 1948; reproduced from *Strong Words, Brave Deeds: The Poetry, Life and Times of Thomas O'Brien* (op. cit.).

Miles Tomalin *To England from the English Dead* page 73
First published in *Volunteer for Liberty*, 7 November 1938.

Clive Branson *England* page 73
Previously unpublished.

Lorenzo Varela (translated by Lon Elliott) *Spain, May 1st* **1938** page 74
Not strictly a poem by an International Brigader, but it was written by a soldier-poet, translated from Spanish by a British volunteer and first appeared in English in the XV Brigade's newspaper, *Volunteer for Liberty*, on 1 May 1938.

Lorenzo Varela (1917-1978) served in the Republican army through most of the war before going into exile in France, Mexico and Argentina from 1939 until 1976. After the war, he wrote in his native Galician as well as Spanish.

The original Spanish version of the poem was first published in the Madrid daily newspaper *Ahora*, organ of the socialist-communist youth movement JSU (Juventudes Socialistas Unificadas), on 1 May 1937 under the title 'Primero de mayo' ('May 1st'). It has five stanzas, compared with Elliott's six:

I
No hay descanso ni paz en esta tierra,
en esta amarga calle señalada,
en estos corazones.
A vosotros, canteros y pastores,
obreros de París, de Londres y del mundo:
¡No hay descanso ni paz en esta tierra!

II
Hombres, trabajadores lo mismo que vosotros,
con yuntas de bueyes iguales que los vuestros.
Con tornos parecidos
o con rebaños llenos también de polvo y de romero,
por el mismo cielo común y parecidas fábricas,
caminan y trabajan infatigablemente.

III
Hombres, trabajadores lo mismo que vosotros,
con hijos tan hermosos
y sábanas tan pobres en lechos parecidos,
y tierno pan, tan oloroso como el vuestro,
pelean y triunfan al pie de los olivos,
en los trigales rubios,
sobre la nieve vieja que duerme entre los pinos.
Bajo un cielo varón, hombres varones,
fuertes y alegres como lo sois vosotros,
dejan en el olvido
el incendio de sus dormitorios y abuelos mutilados.
¡No hay descanso ni paz en esta tierra
que para siempre ha de llamarse España!
Porque somos, hemos de ser, los únicos propietarios del día,
dueños de las ciudades y verdaderos amos de los campos.

IV
Los hombres de las minas.
Los que trabajan en ganados y montes.
Los que hacen el pan y los que lo cultivan.
Los poetas, herreros, leñadores,
el nombre guardan, y la sangre del pueblo
en la quemada tierra de las avanzadillas,
en los talleres.

V
¡No hay descanso ni paz en esta tierra!
Sólo hay flores que viven en tinajas quemadas.
Castas que terminó la Artillería.
Hombres que no descansan,
despiertos siempre, como están los castaños
hasta que la victoria da los frutos.

James R Jump *Shared Cigarette* page 76
First published in *Tribune*, 27 October 1989.
  This is one of a series of poems which Jump wrote about the death of George Jackson, a Cowdenbeath miner who was with the British Battalion's No.2 Machine Gun Company when he was killed, aged 28, on 19 August 1938 in the Sierra de Pandols during the battle of the Ebro. In 1960 Jump met Jackson's brother and niece after he wrote a letter to *Reynolds News*, saying how much the Johnny and the Hurricanes pop hit 'Red River Rock' (to the same 'Red River Valley' tune as 'Jarama Valley') reminded him of his former comrades in Spain such as George Jackson. The brother saw the letter and the newspaper forwarded his message to Jump, who travelled from Kent to Fife to let the family know, after more than 20 years, the details of Jackson's death.

Bill Harrington *Farewell* page 77
First published in *Volunteer for Liberty*, 6 October 1938.

Anonymous *Eyes* page 77
First published in *Poems for Spain* (op. cit.), in which, without further explanation, the poem is attributed to 'Anonymous. International Brigade'.
  However, Rob Stradling, in his *Wales and the Spanish Civil War: The Dragon's Dearest Cause?*, University of Wales Press, Cardiff 2004, ascribes the poem to Jack Roberts: 'Surrounded by noise and horror, pain and death, crouched under a bush at Brunete, Roberts scribbled a few lines of verse which have come to rival WH Auden's ode 'Spain' as the most famous English-language poem of the Spanish Civil War.' Jack 'Russia' Roberts was born in 1899 in Penrhyndeudraeth, then in Merionethshire. He was a Communist local councillor in Caerphilly when he left for Spain in January 1937. He did not join the British Battalion until May, having been arrested and repatriated to Wales on his first attempt to cross France. He was appointed battalion political commissar and saw action at Brunete in July and Quinto in August, where he was wounded in the arm. Following stints in hospital and at the officers' training school at Tarazona de la Mancha, after which he was promoted to lieutenant, he returned to Wales in February 1938. He died in 1979.

Ewart Milne *Song of the Night Market* page 78
From *Poetry and the People*, July 1940.

Clive Branson *The Nightingale* page 78
First published in *The Penguin Book of Spanish Civil War Verse* (op. cit.).
  San Pedro de Cardeña, near Burgos, was the site of a prison camp where Branson and many other captured International Brigaders were held.

Clive Branson *San Pedro* page 79
First published in *New Writing*, spring 1939.

Aileen Palmer *'The dead have no regrets'* page 79
Taken from a photocopied sheet in the Marx Memorial Library, London; reproduced by permission of State Trustees, Victoria.
  Palmer couples the poet and dramatist Frederico García Lorca (see note on page 29) with the German poet Heinrich Heine (1797-1856), whose books were burnt and banned by the Nazis.

David Marshall *Retrospect* page 81
First published in *Poems for Spain* (op. cit.).

Ewart Milne *The Hour Glass (1)* page 82
First published in *Letter from Ireland* (op. cit.).

Clive Branson *On the Statue of the Virgin* page 83
Previously unpublished.

Branson was held by the Italians in a Palencia jail before his release in October 1938.

Anonymous *Salud, Brigade – Salud!* page 83
First published in *Volunteer for Liberty*, April 1940 and perhaps written by a volunteer. An accompanying note says: 'This was sent to us by Tom McWhirter's mother. It was written by a friend of Tom's when he heard of Tom's death at Caspe, in March 1938.' McWhirter, born in 1905, was a carpenter, from Maybole, Ayrshire, who had arrived in Spain in January 1937.

David Marshall *I Sing of my Comrades* page 84
First published in *The Tilting Planet: Poems by David Marshall* (op. cit.).

Tony McLean *'I wept the day that Barcelona fell'* page 85
Previously unpublished.

According to the Bible, Malchus was the High Priest's slave whose ear was cut off by Peter's sword when Jesus was arrested. His ear was healed in Jesus' last miracle before crucifixion.

'Christopher lost, John gone and Edward slain' would refer to the poets Christopher Caudwell (see biographical note on page 28) and John Cornford (see biographical note on page 111) and to Edward Henry Burke. Burke was an actor with the Royal Shakespeare Company, who used the name 'Cooper' in the theatre. He travelled to Spain with Cornford and others in October 1936 and was attached to the Machine Gun Company of the Commune de Paris Battalion, seeing action during the defence of Madrid at University City, Casa de Campo and Boadilla. With the mainly British and Irish No.1 Company of the La Marseillaise Battalion, he was sent to the Córdoba front on Christmas Day and was wounded in the stomach at Lopera two days later. He died of his injuries in a Madrid hospital on 12 February 1937.

Bill Harrington *In an Olive Grove* page 85
First published in *Volunteer for Liberty*, October 1938.

David Martin *Remember* page 86
First published in *Battlefields and Girls: Poems by David Martin*, William MacLellan, Glasgow 1942.

George Nathan, age unknown, from Bethnal Green, east London, an ex-army officer and First World War veteran, was the XV Brigade's chief of operations during the Brunete offensive. He was killed by a shell on 16 July 1937.

Tony McLean *For Antonio Tessaro of Padua, missing in Aragon, 1938* page 87
Previously unpublished.

Antonio Tessaro worked for the municipality of Padua and was a member of the underground Italian Communist Party, which had helped smuggle him out of Italy to join the International Brigades. McLean befriended him in Spain, later recalling that, like other volunteers from countries already under fascist rule, he was not able to write to his parents and 'special channels' had to be found for communicating with home. Tessaro, who spoke a little English, was killed in the retreat through Aragón in the spring of 1938. He was one of hundreds of 'extremely pleasant and brave' men whose deaths in Spain went unrecorded (Tony McLean, Imperial War Museum Sound Archive, London).

Giambettino Cignaroli (1706-1770) and Andrea Mantegna (1431-1506) were Italian painters from the Venice region, of which Padua forms part.

Jim Haughey *Fighter Pilot* page 87
No direct reference to Spain in this poem, but Haughey foretells his death in the continuing war against fascism. It was first published in *The Sunday Times* on 31 October 1943 under the name Seamus Haughey. The poem is reprinted here from the revised edition of *Connolly Column*, by International Brigade veteran Michael O'Riordan, Warren & Pell, Torfaen 2005. O'Riordan, born in Cork in 1917, served in the British Battalion from May to December 1938. He died in 2006.

Anonymous *For Spain and for Sam Wild* page 88
Unattributed, probably previously unpublished poem found among Sam Wild's papers at the Marx Memorial Library, London. Was it written by a fellow International Brigader? Possibly, but it also shares stylistic similarities with poems by Nancy Cunard, who in 1937 famously compiled the *Left Review* pamphlet 'Authors Take Sides on the Spanish War', featuring writers' comments about the war. She visited Republican Spain in 1936 and 1937, reported on the fall of Catalonia for the *Manchester Guardian* in 1939 and after the war campaigned for Spanish refugees and Republican prisoners. However, the poem is not among those which Cunard chose to preserve and which are lodged at the Bodleian Library, Oxford.

Cunard's poem about Franco's deliberate bombardment of civilians, 'To Eat To-day', published in the *New Statesman and Nation* of 1 October 1938, concludes:

On the simple earth
Five mouths less to feed to-night in Barcelona.
On the simple earth
Men trampling and raving on an edge of fear.
Another country arming, another and another behind it –
Europe's nerve strung like catapult, the cataclysms roaring and swelling ...
But in Spain no Perhaps, and To-morrow – in Spain, it is, Here.

Whoever was the author of 'For Spain and for Sam Wild', the poem is worthy of inclusion as a tribute to the former British Battalion commander who was born in Manchester in 1908 and served in the Royal Navy for eleven years before arriving in Spain at the end of December 1936. Wounded at the battle of Jarama in February 1937 and at Brunete in July later that year, he was promoted to No.3 Company commander in January 1938 and to British Battalion commander in February 1938. He was among a group of Britons who escaped after being briefly captured during intense fighting at Caspe, in Aragón, in March 1938. He was yet again injured during the battle of the Ebro six months later. After the Second World War he worked as a steel erector and was active in the Constructional Engineering Union. He died in Manchester in 1983.

Miguel de Cervantes, famous for his novel *Don Quijote de la Mancha*, wrote a play, *La Numancia* (1582), about the fierce resistance to the Romans by the Celtiberians of Numantia (Numantium) in northern Castile from 153 to 133 BC.

David Martin *Jarama* page 89
First published in *Spain Today*, February 1948.

Bert Neville *England, Arise* page 90
First published in *Nineteen Poems*, by Bert Neville, London 1950.

Notes on the poems

Aileen Palmer *Letter from the Underworld* page 91
Published in *Women's Voices from the Spanish Civil War* (op. cit); reproduced by permission of State Trustees, Victoria.

Tony McLean *'Have we no Dante for to-day's Aquinas?'* page 91
Previously unpublished.
The 13th century philosopher Thomas Aquinas, born near Naples, inspired the Renaissance Florentine poet Dante Alighieri, author of *The Divine Comedy*, which was written early in the next century.

Miles Tomalin *Aftermath* page 92
First published in *The Penguin Book of Spanish Civil War Verse* (op. cit).
On 26 April 1937, during Franco's offensive against the Republic's northern enclave, Hitler's Condor Legion attacked and destroyed the Basque town of Guernica in what was the first mass aerial bombing in Europe of a civilian target. The atrocity was reported by George Steer, correspondent of *The Times*, who described how Heinkel fighters plunged low over the town to machine gun civilians who had survived the bombing. Immortalised by the painting by Pablo Picasso, the crime was denied by Franco's supporters both in Spain and abroad until the 1970s. For example, see Brian Crozier's chapter in *The Distant Drum: Reflections on the Spanish Civil War* (op. cit.).
'El Caudillo' was the title, like Mussolini's 'Il Duce' and Hitler's 'Der Führer', chosen by Franco for himself.

Tom Wintringham *Monument* page 93
First published in *Left Review*, October 1937.
General Paul Lukács (Lukacsz in the poem), real name Mata Zalka, was a Hungarian International Brigader killed by a shell near Huesca in June 1937. Buenaventura Durruti (Durrutti in the poem) was an anarchist trade union leader killed during the defence of Madrid in November 1936.

Thomas O'Brien *The Doomed* page 95
First published in *Strong Words, Brave Deeds: The Poetry, Life and Times of Thomas O'Brien* (op. cit).

Bob Cooney *Hasta la Vista, Madrid!* page 96
Written for a reunion of the British Battalion at the Cora Hotel, London, in 1965. It was published in *Bill Feeley: Singer, Steel Erector, International Brigader*, AUEW Constructional Division, Manchester 1978.
The Cliveden Set was the name given to a group of influential politicians and journalists who during the 1930s promoted the policy of appeasement with Hitler. They would meet at the home of Conservative MP Nancy Astor in Cliveden, Buckinghamshire.
'Even in far off Cuba / Men who had learned their craft in Spain' almost certainly refers to Alberto Bayo, the Cuban-born Spanish Republican officer who in the 1950s, while exiled in Mexico, helped to train Fidel Castro's guerillas, then fighting to overthrow Cuban dictator Fulgencio Batista. After the revolution in 1959, Bayo settled in Cuba and became an army general.
António de Oliveira Salazar was the dictator of Portugal from 1932 to 1968 and an ally of Franco.

Bill Feeley *Return to Spain* page 100
Written at the 40th anniversary reunion of International Brigaders at Loughborough Cooperative College in July/August 1976. It was first published in *Greater Manchester*

Men Who Fought in Spain, International Brigade Memorial Committee, Manchester 1983, the commemorative booklet for the unveiling that year of the International Brigade memorial in Manchester Town Hall.

James R Jump *Comrades* page 100
First published in *From Britain to Spain and Back: Poems by Jimmy Jump*, John Cornford Poetry Society, London 1984. It was reprinted a year later in *In Defence of Liberty*, the International Brigade Association's booklet to mark the unveiling of the International Brigade memorial in Jubilee Gardens in London's South Bank.
    Following the death of Franco, Jump lived for a few years in Logroño in the province of La Rioja. From there, he travelled by train down the Ebro valley to Saragossa to meet up with a group of veterans visiting the battlefields of Aragón. This poem describes that encounter.

David Marshall *I Wish I Were Back …* page 102
First published in *The Tilting Planet: Poems by David Marshall* (op. cit.).

Thomas O'Brien *'The deserters, all three, complaining'* page 102
First published in *Strong Words, Brave Deeds: The Poetry, Life and Times of Thomas O'Brien* (op. cit.).

Hugh Sloan *A Tribute* page 104
Previously unpublished.
    The line 'We became one people defending the homes of Spain and our own' recalls the verse written by Sloan's friend, Miles Tomalin, which appeared in the Christmas 1937/New Year 1938 card from the English speaking International Brigade battalions:

He gives, but he has all to gain,
He watches not for Spain alone.
Behind him stand the homes of Spain,
Behind him stands his own.

'There was no other way we could go' echoes the inscription on the International Brigade memorial in London's Jubilee Gardens – 'Our open eyes could see no other way' – taken from C Day Lewis' poem, 'The Volunteer' (quoted on page 19).

Ewart Milne *Channel Spray* page 104
First published in *Drums without End: Stories mainly about the Spanish Civil War* (op. cit.).
    Fianna were legendary Irish warriors of the 3rd century. They gave their name to Fianna Fáil, the republican party of Irish president Eamon de Valera and prime minister Seán Lemass. Basil Brooke was an Ulster Unionist politician and Northern Ireland premier. Charles Parnell campaigned for Irish home rule in the 19th century. The trade union and socialist leader James Connolly, after whom the Irish 'Connolly Column' of the XV Brigade in Spain was named, was executed by the British for his part in the Easter Rising of 1916.

James R Jump *Joe Monks* page 105
First published in *With Machine Gun and Pen* (op. cit.).
    Ralph Fox and John Cornford (see biographical notes on page 26 and page 111 respectively), Frank Conroy, Michael Nolan and Tommy Woods arrived in Spain in December 1936 and were all killed at the Córdoba front while, along with Joe Monks, part of a contingent of British and Irish volunteers in the La Marseillaise Battalion.

Conroy, age unknown, from Kildare but living in London, and Nolan, 26, from Dublin, both Irish Republican Congress Party members, were killed at Lopera on 28 December. Woods, 17, from Dublin, was badly injured on the same day and died in hospital at Andújar on 29 December.

David Marshall *I Have Lived in a Time of Heroes* page 106
First published in *The Tilting Planet: Poems by David Marshall* (op. cit.).

Select index of poets and other British and Irish International Brigaders

Index of poem titles and first lines